To Becoming Financially Whole

Irene Mugure Nderitu

Published by Irene Mugure Nderitu, 2025.

TO BECOMING FINANCIALLY WHOLE

First edition. December 22, 2025.

ISBN: 979-8233081279

Written by Irene Mugure Nderitu.

Table of Contents

DEDICATION

Foremost, to the Almighty God for His gift of Life, Providence, Grace and ordering my steps to the Great Commission.

To my loving and caring Dad, the Late Paul Mwangi Nderito, for being a great role model on financial stewardship.

To my beautiful daughter, Lisa Wabai Nderitu, for bearing it all and helping me unlearn and relearn financial stewardship.

Volume I: The Foundation of Financial Wholeness

Foreword

THE INVITATION TO SACRED Stewardship

My dear fellow traveler on the path of Becoming,

There exists within every human heart a deep longing for wholeness, for the integration of all the fragmented pieces of our lives into a beautiful, cohesive whole. We seek wholeness in our relationships, in our spiritual walk, in our emotional well-being and yet one of the most fundamental areas where wholeness can be cultivated, our financial lives, plagues us so often.

We therefore delve into the sensitive, emotive and sacred space where faith meets finance, where spiritual principles intersect with practical money management. Our exploration into finance is born from the conviction that our financial journey is not separate from our spiritual journey but is indeed an essential expression of it. Just as we explored becoming better versions of ourselves and captains of our souls, we now turn to the transformative work of becoming faithful stewards of all God has entrusted to us.

We will explore together how every financial decision, from the most mundane daily purchase to the most significant investment can become an act of worship, an expression of trust and an opportunity for spiritual growth.

The journey to financial wholeness is ultimately about freedom, the freedom to love generously, to serve joyfully and to live purposefully without the burden of financial anxiety or the distraction of misplaced priorities. It is about discovering that true wealth is not measured by what we accumulate but by what we distribute, not by what we keep but by what we share.

As we embark on this sacred journey together, may you discover the profound peace that comes from aligning our financial practices with our deepest values and spiritual convictions. May we experience the joy of faithful stewardship and the freedom of financial wholeness.

Introduction

THE PARADIGM OF SACRED Stewardship

"The earth is the Lord's and everything in it, the world and all who live in it" as written in Psalm 24:1.

The journey begins with a truth so crucial, so transformative, that it has the power to revolutionize our relationship with money and that truth is that nothing we possess is truly ours.

We are stewards, not owners, we are temporary managers of resources that ultimately belong to God. This paradigm shift from ownership to stewardship represents the foundational stone upon which financial wholeness is built.

In a world that constantly whispers the lie that we are what we possess, that our security lies in our accumulations and that our worth is measured by our wealth, the biblical truth of stewardship comes as liberating news. It frees us from the crushing burden of ownership and invites us into the sacred responsibility of management. When we embrace our identity as stewards rather than owners, every financial decision becomes infused with spiritual significance and every resource becomes an opportunity for faithful service.

This journey toward financial wholeness is not primarily about learning budgeting techniques or investment. It is about the integration of our financial lives with our spiritual values, the alignment of our money habits with our God-given purpose and the transformation of our relationship with resources from one of anxiety to one of trust, from scarcity to abundance, from hoarding to generosity.

We are to explore what it means to be financially whole, what it means to experience peace in our financial lives, to lay emphasis on purpose in our financial decisions and freedom in our financial practices. How financial wholeness enables us to live more fully into all that God has called us to be and to participate more completely in His work of restoration and redemption in the world.

The path to financial wholeness is said to be both practical and spiritual, both individual and communal, both immediate and eternal. It requires honesty about our present reality and hope for our future possibilities. It demands courage to confront our financial patterns and faith to trust God's provision.

IT INVITES US TO BRING our entire selves, our fears and dreams, our failures and aspirations, our practical concerns and spiritual longings into the transformative light of God's wisdom and grace.

As we begin this journey together, may we open our hearts to the possibility that our financial life can become one of the most meaningful arenas of our spiritual growth.

To remain intentional, deliberate and embrace spiritual receptivity. May through this exploration, discover the profound joy and freedom that come from becoming a faithful steward of all God has entrusted to us.

Chapter 1: The Heart of the Steward

CULTIVATING A SPIRIT of Trust and Gratitude

"Keep your lives free from the love of money and be content with what you have, because God has said, "Never will I leave you, never will I forsake you" in Hebrews 13:5.

The journey to financial wholeness begins not with a spreadsheet or a budget but with the human heart. It is in the hidden recesses of our desires, fears and attachments that our financial patterns are born and it is here that transformation must first take place. Before we can change our financial behaviors, we must first examine and transform the inner landscape from which those behaviors emerge.

The Great Lie of Ownership

We live in a culture that worships at the altar of ownership. From childhood, we are taught to believe that security comes from possession, that IDENTITY is found in accumulation and that the goal of life is to build our own little empires of stuff. This mindset of ownership permeates our thinking so deeply that we often fail to recognize it as the source of much of our financial anxiety, distress and discontent.

The paradigm of ownership tells us that what we have is ours to control, to consume, and to protect. In addition, that it is born solely out of our strength and effort.

It breeds anxiety because deep down we know that everything we "own" is temporary, that is, it is subject to loss, decay and ultimately death. It fosters greed because if our security depends on what we possess, and then never can we possess enough. It isolates us because it teaches us to see others as competitors for limited resources rather than as fellow stewards of God's abundant provision.

The biblical worldview offers a radical alternative to this ownership mindset, the paradigm of stewardship. Stewardship recognizes that God is the ultimate owner of all things and we are merely temporary managers of resources that belong to Him. This truth, when fully embraced, has the power to transform our relationship with money from one of anxiety to one of trust, from scarcity to abundance, from grasping to generosity.

THE FREEDOM OF STEWARDSHIP

When we shift from seeing ourselves as owners to understanding ourselves as stewards, several profound transformations occur in our hearts and minds.

First, we experience liberation from anxiety. If the resources we manage ultimately belong to God, then the ultimate responsibility for their provision and protection rests with Him. Our role is not to guarantee outcomes but to exercise faithful management. This does not mean we become passive or irresponsible rather, we engage our responsibilities with diligence while releasing the burden of ultimate control.

Second, we discover freedom from the tyranny of comparison. In the ownership paradigm, we constantly compare our possessions with those of others, leading either to pride or to shame. In the stewardship paradigm, we understand that God has entrusted different resources to different people according to His purposes and their capacities. Our calling is not to have what others have but to be faithful with what we have been given.

Third, we find release from the compulsion to accumulate. When our security rests in God's faithful provision rather than in our accumulations, we are freed from the endless cycle of acquiring more. We can enjoy what we have without being owned by it and we can release it without anxiety when called to do so.

Cultivating a Heart of Gratitude

Gratitude is the natural response of the heart that recognizes everything as gift. When we understand that all we have, that is, our life, our abilities, our resources, our opportunities are expressions of God's grace rather than achievements of our own effort, thankfulness wells up within us. This attitude of gratitude is the antidote to both greed and anxiety.

The practice of gratitude begins with mindfulness, to paying attention to the many gifts that surround us each day. It continues with expression, verbally naming our blessings and giving thanks for them. It also culminates in generosity, sharing freely what we have freely received.

FINANCIAL WHOLENESS flourishes in the soil of gratitude. When we approach our finances with thankful hearts, we make wiser decisions, experience greater contentment and find more joy in both having and sharing. Gratitude transforms budgeting from restrictive accounting to purposeful allocation, saving from anxious hoarding to wise preparation and spending from mindless consumption to values-based stewardship.

Developing Trust in God's Provision

Trust is the cornerstone of the steward's heart. It is the confident assurance that the God who owns everything will provide what we need to fulfill His purposes for our lives. This trust is not passive, it is an active reliance that engages our diligence while resting in God's faithfulness.

Developing trust requires both remembering and rehearsing. We remember God's past faithfulness, recalling specific times when He provided for our needs in surprising or timely ways. We also rehearse trust through present choices, making financial decisions that demonstrate our reliance on God rather than on our own resources alone.

The steward who trusts God's provision can live with open hands, receiving gratefully, holding loosely and giving generously. This posture of trust liberates us from the fear of lack and empowers us to live and give courageously.

Prayer for the Steward's Heart

"Gracious God, owner of all that exists, forgive me for the times I have lived as an owner rather than a steward. Help me to release the burden of control and to trust in your faithful provision. Cultivate in me a heart of gratitude that recognizes every good gift as coming from you. Transform my relationship with money from one of anxiety to one of trust, from scarcity to abundance, from grasping to generosity. May my financial life become an expression of my love for you and my trust in your care. Amen".

WORKSHEET 1.1: EXAMINING Your Money Mindset

Purpose: To identify and transform deeply held beliefs about money that may be hindering your journey toward financial wholeness.

Section A: Reflection Questions

1. What messages about money did you receive from your family while growing up?
2. What emotions do you typically feel when you think about money? For instance, anxiety, distress, guilt, shame, confidence and or peace.
3. Complete this sentence: "If I had more money, I would finally..."
4. What do you believe about God's role in your financial life?
5. How does your current financial situation affect your sense of self-worth?

Section B: Identifying Limiting Beliefs

List any beliefs about money that may be limiting your financial wholeness. For instance, "There will never be enough" "Money is the root of all evil" "Rich people are greedy"

1.
2.
3.

Now, reframe each limiting belief with a stewardship perspective;

1.
2.
3.

Section C: Gratitude Practice

List 10 financial blessings in your life right now, no matter how small;

1.
2.
3.
4.
5.
6.
7.
8.
9.
10.

Section D: Commitment Statement

Write a personal commitment to developing a steward's mindset;

"I, ____________________, commit to cultivating a heart of trust and gratitude in my financial life. I recognize that all I have belongs to God and I am called to be a faithful steward. I release the burden of ownership and embrace the freedom of stewardship".

Signed: ____________________ Date: ____________________

Journal Prompt 1.1: The Steward's Reflection

Take 15-20 minutes to reflect on the following questions in your financial wholeness journal;

1. How would my financial decisions change if I truly believed that everything I have belongs to God?
2. What specific anxieties about money do I need to release to God today?
3. Where have I seen evidence of God's provision in my financial life recently?
4. What is the one-step I can take this week to move from an ownership mindset to a stewardship mindset?

Chapter 2: Discovering Your Divine Assignment

ALIGNING FINANCES WITH Purpose

"For we are God's handiwork, created in Christ Jesus to do good works, which God prepared in advance for us to do" as written in Ephesians 2:10.

Financial management becomes soul draining when disconnected from deeper purpose. Why do we seek financial stability? For what purpose do we allocate resources? The answers to these questions determine whether our financial practices will lead to life or to mere existence. Each of us carries a unique divine assignment, a specific contribution we are called to make in this world. Our financial decisions should fuel this mission rather than distract from it.

The Quest for Purpose

Human beings are purpose-seeking creatures. We long for our lives to matter, to have meaning, for our existence to make a difference in the world.

This longing is not accidental, a purposeful Creator weaves it into the fabric of our being. When our financial lives are disconnected from this deeper sense of purpose, money becomes either a meaningless distraction or an idolatrous pursuit.

Discovering our divine assignment involves listening for the unique ways God has wired us to participate in His work of restoration and redemption in the world. It requires paying attention to the things that make our hearts come alive, the needs that stir our compassion, the abilities that come naturally to us and the opportunities that consistently present themselves to us.

Our divine assignment is not necessarily our job title, though it may find expression through our work. It is the essential contribution we are called to make, that is, for the specific good works God prepared in advance for us to do.

When our financial decisions are aligned with this assignment, money becomes a tool for meaning rather than an end in itself.

From Purpose to Financial Mission

Once we have clarity about our divine assignment, the next step is to translate that purpose into a financial mission statement. This statement serves as a guiding light for our financial decisions, helping us to allocate resources in ways that support rather than undermine our core calling.

A financial mission statement typically includes;

- Your understanding of your divine assignment
- The values that will guide your financial decisions
- The financial goals that will enable you to fulfill your purpose
- The boundaries that will protect you from distractions

For example, if your divine assignment involves hospitality and creating spaces where people experience belonging, your financial mission might include prioritizing housing that enables generous entertainment, budgeting for food and hospitality expenses and perhaps even saving for a larger home or a retreat space.

If your assignment involves advocacy for the marginalized, your financial mission might include intentional spending with ethical companies, generous giving to organizations that serve the poor and career choices that prioritize impact over income.

Values-Based Financial Decision Making

When our financial decisions are guided by a clear sense of purpose and mission, every spending choice becomes an opportunity to express your values. Values-based decision making involves asking not just "Can I afford this?" but also "Does this purchase align with my values and support my divine assignment?"

This approach transforms budgeting from restrictive accounting to intentional value expression. Instead of feeling limited by a budget, one experiences the freedom of funding what matters most to you. Your spending plan becomes a tangible expression of your deepest convictions and commitments.

VALUES-BASED DECISION making also provides clarity when faced with financial trade-offs. When you know what matters most, it becomes easier to say no to good opportunities in order to say yes to the best ones. It helps you distinguish between wants that are merely attractive and wants that are aligned with your purpose.

Prayer for Purpose and Mission

"Loving God, creator of all that is and author of my life, thank you for creating me with a unique purpose and calling. Reveal to me the specific good works you prepared in advance for me to do. Grant me clarity about my divine assignment and wisdom to align my financial life with it. Help me to use the resources you have entrusted to me to fuel your purposes in the world. May my financial decisions reflect my values and support my calling. Amen".

Worksheet 2.1: Discovering Your Divine Assignment

Purpose: To identify your core purpose and translate it into a financial mission statement.

Section A: Purpose Discovery

1. What makes your heart come alive? What activities cause you to lose track of time?
2. What needs in the world stir your compassion or righteous anger?
3. What unique abilities has God given you? What do people often ask you for help with?
4. What opportunities consistently present themselves to you?
5. If money were no object, how would you spend your time serving others?

Section B: Financial Mission Statement

Based on your reflections above, draft your financial mission statement:

"My financial mission is to steward God's resources in a way that supports my calling to ______________________________. I will prioritize financial decisions that align with my values of ______________________________ and enable me to ______________________________."

Section C: Alignment Assessment

Rate your current financial practices on a scale of 1-10 (1 = not aligned, 10 = fully aligned) with your divine assignment:

- Spending habits: _____
- Saving goals: _____
- Giving patterns: _____
- Career choices: _____
- Investment decisions: _____

Section D: Action Steps

List three specific changes you will make to better align your finances with your purpose:

1.
2.
3.

Journal Prompt 2.1: Purpose and Provision

Reflect on these questions in your journal:

1. How has God provided resources for me to fulfill aspects of my calling in the past?
2. What financial fears or obstacles currently prevent me from fully pursuing my divine assignment?
3. How might my financial decisions look different if I truly believed God would provide what I need to fulfill His purposes for my life?

Chapter 3: The Steward's Compass

CREATING A VALUES-BASED Financial Plan

In Luke 14:28 we are reminded, "Suppose one of you wants to build a tower. Will you not first sit down and estimate the cost to see if you have enough money to complete it?"

With that in mind and having a clear understanding of our identity as stewards of our divine assignment, we now turn to the practical work of financial planning.

A values-based financial plan serves as the steward's compass, guiding our financial decisions in alignment with our purpose and values.

Unlike conventional budgeting that often feels restrictive, values-based financial planning is an empowering process that ensures our money serves our deepest convictions rather than controlling us.

The Philosophy of Values-Based Planning

Values-based financial planning begins with the recognition that money is a tool, not a goal. Its purpose is to support the life we feel called to live, a life of purpose, meaning and service. This approach to financial planning asks not "How much money do I need?" but rather "What life am I called to live and how can money support that calling?"

This philosophy stands in stark contrast to the world's approach to money, which typically involves setting financial targets based on comparison with others or arbitrary standards of success. Values-based planning, by contrast, involves listening to God's unique calling for our lives and then designing a financial plan that supports that calling.

The process involves several key components, that is, clarifying our values, setting goals that reflect those values, creating a spending plan that funds what matters most and establishing systems that make values-based decisions automatic.

Clarifying Core Values

Our values are the principles that guide our decisions and shape our lives. They represent what matters most to us, the ideals we want to characterize our lives and the legacy we hope to leave. Clarifying our core values is an essential step in values-based financial planning, as these values will serve as the foundation for all our financial decisions.

Common values that might guide financial decisions include;

- **Generosity:** Reflected in generous giving to church, charity and individuals in need
- **Hospitality:** Expressed through budgeting for entertainment, meals and housing that enables welcoming others
- **Justice:** Demonstrated through ethical spending, investing and career choices
- **Learning:** Prioritized through education savings and spending on personal growth
- **Family:** Reflected in decisions that prioritize time with loved ones
- **Simplicity:** Expressed through intentional limitation of possessions and expenses

The process of clarifying values involves both reflection and prayer. We look back at our lives to identify times when we felt most fulfilled and aligned, examining what values were being expressed in those moments.

We therefore plan and look forward, in consideration of what values we want to characterize our lives in the years to come and the legacy we hope to leave behind.

From Values to Financial Goals

Once we have clarity about our core values, the next step is to translate those values into specific financial goals. These goals become the tangible expression of our values, the specific ways we will use financial resources to support what matters most to us.

FOR EXAMPLE, IF ONE of our core values is generosity, our financial goals might include;

- Giving 10% of our income to our local church
- Setting aside 5% of our income for spontaneous giving opportunities
- Building a generosity fund that enables us to respond to larger needs

If simplicity is a core value, our goals might include;

- Paying off all consumer debt within 24 months
- Reducing our monthly expenses by 15% to create more margin
- Saving for a smaller, more manageable home

We have to keep in mind that well-crafted financial goals are SMART, that is, Specific, Measurable, Achievable, Relevant and Time-bound. SMART goals provide clear direction for our financial decisions and motivate us to stay the course when temptations arise.

Creating a Values-Based Spending Plan

A values-based spending plan is the practical tool that ensures our money actually goes toward what we value most. Unlike traditional budgets that often feel like straitjackets, a values-based spending plan feels like a declaration of freedom, it is our intentional plan to fund what matters most to us.

The process of creating a values-based spending plan involves;

1. Identifying our income from all sources
2. Allocating funds to our highest priorities first such as giving, saving and or debt repayment
3. Distributing remaining funds to other categories based on our values
4. Ensuring our spending aligns with our values and goals

The key difference between a values-based spending plan and a conventional budget is the order of operations. Conventional budgeting often involves tracking where our money is going and then trying to cut back. Values-based planning involves deciding where we want our money to go based on our values and then making adjustments to ensure it goes there.

Systems for Success

Creating a values-based financial plan is important, but implementing it consistently is what produces results. This requires developing systems that make values-based decisions automatic and easy.

Helpful systems include;

- Automated transfers for giving, saving and investing
- Regular financial check-ins to review progress and make adjustments
- Accountability partnerships with like-minded stewards
- Visual reminders of our values and goals
- Pre-commitment strategies for potential temptation areas

These systems reduce our reliance on willpower alone and create an environment that supports our values-based financial decisions.

Prayer for Financial Planning

"Wisdom-giving God, Grant me clarity about the values you want to characterize my life. Give me wisdom to set financial goals that reflect your purposes for me. Help me create a financial plan that honors you and serves others. Grant me discipline to follow through on my commitments and grace to adjust when circumstances change.

May my financial planning be an act of worship and trust. Amen".

WORKSHEET 3.1: VALUES-Based Financial Planning

Purpose: To create a comprehensive financial plan based on your core values and divine assignment.

Section A: Values Identification

List your top 5-7 core values such as generosity, hospitality, justice, learning, family, simplicity;

1.
2.
3.
4.
5.
6.
7.

For each value, write one sentence about how it should impact your financial decisions;

SECTION B: FINANCIAL Goals Setting

Based on your values, set 3-5 financial goals for the next year:

1.
2.
3.
4.
5.

Set 3-5 financial goals for the next 5-10 years:

1.
2.
3.
4.
5.

Section C: Spending Plan Template

Monthly Income: $_________

Values-Based Allocation:

- Giving: $_________ (%)
- Saving/Investing: $_________ (%)
- Debt Repayment: $_________ (%)
- Housing: $_________ (%)
- Transportation: $_________ (%)
- Food: $_________ (%)
-

Total: $_________ (100%)

Section D: Implementation Systems

What systems will you put in place to ensure you follow your values-based plan?

- Automated transfers:
- Accountability partners:
- Regular check-ins:
- Visual reminders:
- Other systems:

Journal Prompt 3.1: Values and Money

Reflect on these questions;

1. Where do I see tension between my stated values and my actual spending patterns?
2. What one change in my spending would most significantly align my money with my values?

3. How can I create more margin in my finances to fund what matters most?

Volume II: Practical Pathways to Financial Freedom

Chapter 4: The Debt-Free Journey

BREAKING CHAINS AND Finding Financial Liberty

In Proverbs 22:7, it is written, "The rich rule over the poor and the borrower is slave to the lender".

Debt represents one of the most significant obstacles to financial wholeness in our modern world. It chains us to past decisions, limits our present choices and mortgages our future possibilities. Yet for many, debt feels like an inescapable reality, unavoidable in a world of rising costs and stagnant wages. Thus, the need to explore on how to break free from the bondage of debt and walk in the financial liberty God intends for His children.

Understanding Debt's True Cost

Debt's cost extends far beyond the interest rates printed on statements. The true cost of debt includes:

- **Spiritual Cost**

Debt often reflects and reinforces a lack of trust in God's provision. It can become a substitute for patience and a barrier to generosity.

- **Emotional Cost**

The stress of debt burdens relationships affects health and clouds our ability to hear God's guidance.

- **Opportunity Cost**

Money spent on debt payments cannot be used for God's kingdom purposes, personal growth or helping others.

- **Relational Cost**

Financial pressure from debt strains marriages, families and friendships.

When we understand debt's comprehensive cost, we recognize that becoming debt-free is not just about improving our financial situation, it is about reclaiming our spiritual, emotional and relational freedom.

Biblical Perspective on Debt

While Scripture does not explicitly forbid all borrowing, it consistently presents debt as something to be avoided when possible and quickly eliminated where and when necessary. The Hebrew word for "debt" is closely related to the word for "slavery" revealing how biblical authors understood indebtedness.

Key biblical principles regarding debt include;

- Debt assumes tomorrow's productivity (Proverbs 27:1)
- Debt presumes upon the future (James 4:13-15)
- Debt can hinder our ability to respond to God's promptings
- Debt often reflects impatience or discontentment

Understanding these principles helps us develop a biblical approach to debt elimination that addresses not just the practical but also the spiritual dimensions of our indebtedness.

The Debt Elimination Strategy

Becoming debt-free requires both a strategic approach and spiritual fortitude. The following methods should be explored including others in an effort to achieve debt freedom;

1. **The Debt Inventory**

Create a comprehensive list of all debts, including creditor names, balances, interest rates and minimum payments.

1. **The Emergency Fund**

Before aggressive debt repayment, save a small emergency fund of $1,000-2,000 to prevent new debt when unexpected expenses arise.

1. **The Debt Snowball**

List debts from smallest to largest balance. Make minimum payments on all debts except the smallest, which you attack with intensity. Once the smallest debt is paid, roll its payment into attacking the next smallest debt.

1. **The Intensity Factor**

Temporarily reduce discretionary spending and find ways to increase income to accelerate debt repayment.

1. **The Celebration Plan**

Celebrate each paid-off debt as a milestone victory, thanking God for each step toward freedom.

While some argue for paying highest-interest debts first, the debt snowball method provides psychological wins that build momentum and increase the likelihood of completing the journey to debt freedom.

Addressing the Root Causes

Eliminating existing debt is crucial, but preventing future debt requires addressing the root causes that led to indebtedness. Common root causes include;

- **Lack of Emergency Savings**

Without a financial cushion, unexpected expenses become new debts.

- **Impulse Spending**

Emotional spending or lack of discipline in wants versus needs.

- **Lifestyle Inflation**

Increasing spending as income increases rather than saving the difference.

- **Poor Communication**

In marriages, lack of unified financial vision and accountability.

- **Unexpected Emergencies such as Medical Crises**

Unexpected health issues without adequate insurance.

- **Psychological and emotional issues**

Personal issues on self-worth, love, acceptance and or validation.

Identifying and addressing these root causes is essential for maintaining debt freedom long-term.

Prayer for Debt Freedom

"Liberating God, You desire freedom for your children in every area of life. I bring my debt before you, the financial chains that limit my ability to serve you fully. Give me wisdom to create and follow a debt elimination plan. Grant me discipline to make difficult short-term choices for long-term freedom. Help me address the heart issues that led to debt. Provide creative ways to increase income and decrease expenses.

As I experience debt freedom, use my story to encourage others. Thank you for your provision and deliverance. Amen".

Worksheet 4.1: Debt Inventory and Elimination Plan

Purpose: To create a comprehensive overview of your debt situation and a strategic plan for becoming debt-free.

Section A: Complete Debt Inventory

Creditor	Balance	Interest Rate	Minimum Payment
Totals			

SECTION B: DEBT SNOWBALL Setup

List debts in order from smallest to largest balance:

1. ______________________ Balance: $___________
2. ______________________ Balance: $___________
3. ______________________ Balance: $___________
4. ______________________ Balance: $___________
5. ______________________ Balance: $___________

Section C: Accelerated Payment Plan

Current total minimum payments: $___________

Additional monthly amount I can apply to debt: $___________

Total monthly debt repayment: $___________

Estimated debt-free date: ______________________

Section D: Root Cause Analysis

What factors contributed to my current debt situation?

- Lack of emergency fund
- Medical expenses
- Overspending
- Impulse buying
- Income reduction
- Inadequate insurance
- Other: ______________________

WHAT CHANGES WILL I make to prevent future debt?

1.
2.
3.

Journal Prompt 4.1: Debt and Freedom

Reflect on these questions;

1. How does debt currently limit my ability to serve God and others?
2. What emotions do I feel when I think about my debt? How can I bring these to God?
3. What would financial freedom enable me to do that I cannot do now?

Chapter 5: The Wisdom of Saving

PREPARING FOR TOMORROW While Trusting Today

In Proverbs 21:20, we are reminded "In the house of the wise are stores of choice food and oil but a foolish man devours all he has".

It can therefore be deduced that saving is an act of both wisdom and faith, that is, wisdom in preparing for future needs and faith in God's ongoing provision. In a culture of instant gratification, saving represents a countercultural practice of patience and trust. It demonstrates our belief that God has a future for us worth preparing for and our commitment to be ready for whatever assignment He may give.

The Theology of Saving

Some Christians struggle with saving, wondering if it demonstrates lack of trust in God's provision. However, Scripture consistently commends the practice of saving and preparation;

- Joseph saved during years of plenty to prepare for years of famine (Genesis 41)
- The ant stores provisions in summer for winter needs (Proverbs 6:6-8)
- Parents are to save for their children (2 Corinthians 12:14)

Saving becomes problematic when it crosses into hoarding, that is, when our accumulated resources become a source of security rather than God Himself.

The key is maintaining open hands, saving generously while holding resources loosely, ready to deploy them for God's purposes.

Types of Savings

Biblical saving encompasses multiple dimensions, each serving different purposes;

1. **Emergency Fund**

3-6 months of essential expenses to cover unexpected events without going into debt.

1. **Opportunity Fund**

Resources set aside to capitalize on God-given opportunities such as ministry needs, business ventures or special missions.

1. **Purchase Savings**

Planning for anticipated expenses like vehicles, home repairs or education to avoid future debt.

1. **Generosity Fund**

Building capacity for larger giving opportunities beyond regular tithing.

1. **Retirement Savings**

Preparing for seasons when we may be less able to generate income.

Each type of saving reflects a different aspect of faithful stewardship and requires different strategies and time horizons.

The Savings Hierarchy

When resources are limited, knowing what to save for first is crucial. The following hierarchy provides guidance:

1. **Starter Emergency Fund** ($1,000-2,000)
2. **Debt Elimination** (except mortgage)

3. **Full Emergency Fund** (3-6 months of expenses)
4. **Long-Term Savings and Investing** (15% of income)
5. **Accelerated Wealth Building**

This progression ensures that you are protected against setbacks while systematically building toward financial freedom.

Practical Saving Strategies

Effective saving requires both intention and systemization;

- **Pay Yourself First**

Treat saving like a mandatory bill, the first check you write each month.

- **Automate Transfers**

Set up automatic transfers to savings accounts to remove reliance on willpower.

- **Save Windfalls**

Commit to saving tax refunds, bonuses or unexpected income.

- **Make Saving Visible**

Use visual trackers to maintain motivation and celebrate progress.

- **Start Small**

Even $25 per month builds the savings habit and grows over time.

The key is developing the habit of saving regularly, regardless of the amount.

Trusting God While Saving

The tension between saving wisely and trusting God completely requires ongoing spiritual attention. Helpful practices include;

- **Regular Reflection**: Periodically examining our motives for saving
- **Generous Giving**: Maintaining generous giving even while building savings
- **Flexible Planning**: Holding our savings plans with open hands before God
- **Gratitude Practice**: Thanking God for the ability to save and His provision

When approached with the right heart, saving becomes an act of worship, a practical expression of our trust in God's future faithfulness.

Prayer for Saving Wisdom

"Provider God, You own all things and faithfully provide for your children. Give me wisdom to save appropriately, neither hoarding out of fear nor spending irresponsibly. Help me balance present needs with future preparation. Grant me discipline to save consistently and creativity to find new ways to build reserves. Keep my heart from finding security in accumulated resources rather than in you. May my saving practices honor you and position me to serve your purposes. Amen".

Worksheet 5.1: Savings Goals and Strategy

Purpose: To establish comprehensive savings goals and create a plan to achieve them.

Section A: Savings Priority Assessment

Rate the importance of each savings type for your current situation (1-5, with 5 being most important);

- Emergency Fund: _____
- Opportunity Fund: _____
- Purchase Savings: _____
- Generosity Fund: _____
- Retirement Savings: _____

Section B: Specific Savings Goals

Savings Category	Target Amount	Deadline	Monthly Amount Needed
Emergency Fund			
Total Monthly Savings			

Section C: Savings Systems

How will I automate and systematize my saving?

- Automatic transfers: $__________ on __________ (date) each month
- Accounts needed: __________________________
- Accountability: __________________________

Section D: Progress Tracking

Create a visual tracker for your primary savings goal

(Visual progress chart to be completed each month)

Journal Prompt 5.1: Saving and Trust

Reflect on these questions;

1. What fears or concerns come up when I think about saving money?
2. How can I maintain trust in God's provision while being responsible to save?
3. What future opportunities might God be preparing me for through saving?

Chapter 6: Understanding Credit Wisely

NAVIGATING THE PLASTIC Jungle

"Let no debt remain outstanding, except the continuing debt to love one another" as prescribed in Romans 13:8.

Credit, particularly in the form of credit cards, represents both a useful financial tool and a potential trap. Used wisely, credit can provide convenience, protection and even rewards. Used poorly, it becomes an instrument of bondage. Hence, the need to explore on ways to navigate the world of credit with wisdom and discernment.

The Purpose and Peril of Credit

Credit serves several legitimate purposes;

- **Convenience**: Simplifying transactions, especially online
- **Protection**: Fraud protection and purchase insurance
- **Record Keeping**: Creating a paper trail of expenses
- **Building Credit History**: Establishing a pattern of responsible borrowing

However, credit cards specifically present unique dangers;

- **Decoupling Spending from Pain**

The psychological distance between spending and payment

- **Minimum Payment Trap**

The illusion that small payments mean affordable debt

- **Rewards Temptation**

The danger of overspending to earn rewards

- **Compound Interest Reversal**

Working against you rather than for you

UNDERSTANDING BOTH the benefits and dangers helps us develop a wise approach to credit use.

Biblical Principles for Credit Use

While Scripture does not specifically address modern credit systems, several principles apply;

1. **Debt Avoidance**

"The wicked borrow and do not repay" (Psalm 37:21)

1. **Contentment**

"Godliness with contentment is great gain" (1 Timothy 6:6)

1. **Future Orientation**

"Count the cost" before building (Luke 14:28)

1. **Honoring Commitments**

"When you make a vow to God, do not delay to fulfill it" (Ecclesiastes 5:4)

These principles suggest that while credit use is not inherently sinful, it requires extraordinary wisdom and self-control to use without violating biblical values.

Wisdom-Based Credit Practices

For those who choose to use credit cards, these practices promote wisdom;

1. **Treat Like Debit**

Only charge what you can pay in full each month

1. **Pay Weekly**

Make payments throughout the month to maintain awareness

1. **Set Usage Limits**

Decide maximum charges before the month begins

1. **Automate Full Payment**

Set up automatic full balance payment each month

1. **Regular Evaluation**

Quarterly review of whether credit use still makes sense

Additionally, consider using credit cards only for specific budgeted categories rather than general spending.

Credit Card Debt Recovery

If you are already carrying credit card debt;

1. **Stop Using Cards**: Prevent the problem from worsening
2. **Implement Debt Snowball**
3. **Consider Balance Transfers**: Only if you will not run up new debt
4. **Seek Credit Counseling**: If overwhelmed, consult a reputable nonprofit agency
5. **Communicate with Creditors**: They may offer hardship programs

The key is addressing credit card debt aggressively while changing the habits that created it.

Alternative Approaches

Some stewards find these approaches helpful:

- **The Debit-Only Approach**: Using only debit cards for all transactions
- **The Cash Envelope System**: Using cash for discretionary categories
- **The One-Card Approach**: Maintaining a single credit card for specific uses
- **The Credit-Abstinence Season**: Taking a 3-6 month break from all credit use

THE RIGHT APPROACH depends on your personality, spending tendencies and spiritual convictions.

Prayer for Credit Wisdom

"All-knowing God, You see all things and understand every motive. Give me wisdom to navigate the world of credit with discernment. Protect me from the deception that I can spend tomorrow's money today. Grant me self-control to use credit as a tool rather than a crutch. If credit hinders my financial wholeness, give me courage and strength to eliminate it. May my financial practices reflect your wisdom and honor your name. Amen".

Worksheet 6.1: Credit Assessment and Strategy

Purpose: To evaluate current credit use and establish wise boundaries.

Section A: Current Credit Inventory

Card/Account	Balance	Limit	Interest Rate	Monthly Payment
Totals				

Credit Utilization Ratio (Total Balances/Total Limits): ___________%

Section B: Credit Use Evaluation

Do I carry a balance month-to-month? [ ] Yes [ ] No

If yes, what spending created this debt? ______________________________

Do the benefits of my credit use outweigh the costs? [ ] Yes [ ] No

Why or why not? ______________________________

SECTION C: CREDIT STRATEGY

My approach to credit will be

[ ] Credit card-free

[ ] One card for specific uses

[ ] Multiple cards with careful management

[ ] Other: ____________________________

My credit boundaries;

- Maximum monthly charges: $___________
- Categories I will use credit for: ____________________________
- Payment schedule: ____________________________

Section D: Debt Elimination Plan

If carrying credit card debt, list cards in debt snowball order;

1. ______________________ Balance: $___________
2. ______________________ Balance: $___________
3. ______________________ Balance: $___________

Journal Prompt 6.1: Credit and Contentment

Reflect on these questions;

1. How does credit card use affect my awareness of spending?
2. What emotions do I experience when using credit versus cash?
3. How might my spending patterns change if I used only debit or cash?

Chapter 7: The Steward's Safety Net

INSURANCE AND RISK Management

We are reminded in Proverbs 27:12 that "The prudent see danger and take refuge but the simple keep going and pay the penalty".

Hence the need to consider uptake of Insurance. Insurance represents a practical expression of wisdom and love. Wisdom in preparing for potential dangers and love in protecting those who depend on us. While our ultimate trust remains in God's protection, insurance serves as a tool for responsible stewardship in a fallen world where unexpected events occur.

The Theology of Insurance

Some Christians struggle with insurance, wondering if purchasing protection demonstrates lack of faith.

However, Scripture consistently commends prudence and preparation;

- Noah built an ark to protect against coming judgment (Genesis 6)
- Joseph stored grain to prepare for famine (Genesis 41)
- The wise man builds his house on the rock (Matthew 7:24-27)

Insurance only becomes problematic when we trust in it rather than in God or when it becomes so expensive that it hinders our ability to be generous. The key is maintaining proper perspective, which see insurance as a tool rather than a savior.

Types of Essential Insurance

1. **Health Insurance**

Protection against medical expenses that could otherwise be a financial burden.

1. **Auto Insurance**

Required by law and necessary for protection against liability and repair costs.

1. **Homeowners/Renters Insurance**:

Financial protection in the event of loss/disaster to the dwelling and or household possessions.

1. **Life Insurance**

Essential if others depend on your income.

1. **Disability Insurance**

Protection against loss of income due to injury/incapacity especially given that it is statistically more likely than premature death.

Each type of insurance addresses specific risks that could derail financial stability and hinder our ability to fulfill our stewardship responsibilities.

Determining Appropriate Coverage

Appropriate insurance coverage balances several factors;

- **Risk Tolerance**

How much potential loss can you absorb without financial catastrophe?

- **Dependents**

How many people rely on your income or care?

- **Assets**

What property needs protection?

- **Stage of Life**

Different life stages require different coverage types and amounts

A key and helpful principle to consider is to insure against catastrophes you cannot afford, not inconveniences you can.

INSURANCE AND STEWARDSHIP

Viewing insurance through the lens of stewardship transforms it from unavoidable to an act of love and responsibility;

- **Love for Family**

Ensuring your family would not face financial hardship if something happened to you

- **Responsibility to Creditors**

Honoring commitments even through unexpected events

- **Community Care**

Preventing medical debt that might burden others

- **Ministry Protection**

Ensuring unexpected events do not hinder your ability to serve

This perspective helps us make wise insurance decisions that honor God and serve others.

Practical Insurance Planning

Implementing wise insurance coverage involves;

1. **Annual Review**: Assessing coverage needs each year as circumstances

change

2. **Comparison Shopping**: Ensuring you are getting appropriate coverage at fair prices
3. **Deductible Optimization**: Choosing deductibles that balance premium costs and out-of-pocket risk
4. **Professional Advice**: Consulting with trustworthy insurance professionals when needed
5. **Company Research**: Selecting reputable companies with strong financial ratings

REMEMBER THAT THE CHEAPEST policy is not necessarily the best value if it leaves significant gaps in coverage.

Prayer for Protection and Wisdom

"Protector God, You are our ultimate shield and defender. Give us wisdom to be prudent in managing risks without trusting in our preparations. Help us balance the cost of insurance with our ability to be generous. Guide us to appropriate coverage that protects our families and honors you. Keep our hearts from fear as we take practical steps of preparation. May our insurance decisions reflect both wisdom and trust in you. Amen".

Worksheet 7.1: Insurance Inventory and Assessment

Purpose: To evaluate current insurance coverage and identify needed adjustments.

Section A: Current Coverage Inventory

Insurance Type	Company	Coverage Amount	Premium	Renewal Date
Health				
Auto				
Home/Rental				
Life				
Disability				
Other				

SECTION B: COVERAGE Adequacy Assessment

For each insurance type, rate your current coverage (1 = inadequate, 5 = optimal):

- Health Insurance: _____
- Auto Insurance: _____
- Home/Rental Insurance: _____
- Life Insurance: _____
- Disability Insurance: _____

Section C: Action Steps

Based on your assessment, what insurance adjustments are needed?

1.
2.
3.

Section D: Professional Consultation

What insurance questions do I need to discuss with a professional?

1.
2.

Journal Prompt 7.1: Insurance and Trust

Reflect on these questions:

1. How do I balance trusting God's protection with taking practical steps like purchasing insurance?
2. What fears or concerns come up when I think about potential risks?
3. How can I use insurance as a tool for responsible stewardship rather than a substitute for trust in God?

Volume III: Growing Your Stewardship

Chapter 8: The Art of Skillful Contribution

ADDING VALUE TO SELF and Community

Scripture tells us in Proverbs 22:29 that "Do you see someone skilled in their work? They will serve before kings, they will not serve before officials of low rank".

True prosperity involves expanding our capacity to contribute value to the world. The development of our skills represents an essential dimension of financial wholeness, that is, not merely for increased earning potential but also for the increased ability to serve others effectively.

As we hone our abilities, we become more useful instruments in God's hands, capable of addressing complex needs with excellence and wisdom.

The Theology of Skill Development

Our skills and talents are not accidental, they are God's gracious endowment, designed for both our fulfillment and others' benefit.

The Parable of the Talents in Matthew 25:14-30 reveals that God expects us to develop what He has entrusted to us. Skill development is thus a spiritual discipline, a way of honoring the Giver by maximizing His gifts.

This commitment to skill development should be guided by two questions;

1. What abilities has God given me that, when developed, will allow me to serve others more effectively?
2. What needs exist in my community that require skills I could develop? The pursuit of mastery becomes a spiritual practice when

undertaken for the purpose of increased contribution rather than personal advancement alone.

Identifying Your Unique Skill Set

Each person possesses a unique combination of;

- **Natural Talents**

Abilities that come easily to you

- **Acquired Skills**

Competencies developed through practice and study

- **Spiritual Gifts**

Supernatural gifts given by the Holy Spirit

- **Experiential Wisdom**

Knowledge gained through life experiences

The intersection of these areas represents your unique contribution capacity. Identifying this intersection requires honest self-assessment, feedback from others who know you well and prayerful reflection on what activities bring you joy and fulfillment while serving others.

The Skill Development Pathway

Intentional skill development follows a deliberate pathway;

1. **Assessment**: Honestly evaluating current skill levels and identifying gaps
2. **Goal Setting**: Defining specific competencies to develop
3. **Learning Plan**: Creating a structured approach to skill acquisition
4. **Practice**: Implementing deliberate practice with feedback
5. **Application**: Using new skills in real-world contexts
6. **Refinement**: Continuously improving based on experience

This process transforms vague aspirations for self-improvement into concrete growth that enhances your capacity to serve.

Skill Development and Multiple Income Streams

As you develop valuable skills, you naturally create opportunities for multiple income streams. These might include;

- **Primary Employment**: Using developed skills in your main vocation
- **Consulting**: Offering expert advice in your area of competence
- **Teaching**: Sharing your knowledge through classes or mentoring
- **Product Creation**: Developing resources that help others
- **Freelancing**: Taking on project-based work in your skill area

Multiple income streams not only provide financial resilience but also create more avenues for meaningful contribution.

Community Impact Through Skillful Service

Your developed skills become channels for community impact when you;

- **Identify Real Needs**: Listen to your community to understand actual rather than perceived needs
- **Offer Pro Bono Service**: Volunteer your expertise to organizations that could not otherwise afford it
- **Mentor Others**: Invest in developing skills in the next generation
- **Create Solutions**: Develop products, services or systems that address community challenges
- **Collaborate**: Partner with others whose skills complement yours

This approach transforms skill development from self-focused advancement to community-focused service.

Prayer for Skillful Contribution

"Master Craftsman, You have fearfully and wonderfully made each of us with unique capacities. Reveal the skills and talents you have placed within us. Give us wisdom to develop them for your glory and others' good. Guide me to opportunities where our skills can meet real needs. Keep us from selfish ambition even as we pursue growth. May our developed abilities become channels of your grace to others. Amen".

Worksheet 8.1: Skill Assessment and Development Plan

Purpose: To identify your current skills and create a plan for strategic development.

Section A: Current Skill Inventory

Natural Talents (What comes easily to you)

1.
2.
3.

Acquired Skills (What you have learned to do well)

1.
2.
3.

Spiritual Gifts (Supernatural gifts)

1.
2.
3.

Experiential Wisdom (Knowledge from life experience):

1.
2.
3.

SECTION B: SKILL DEVELOPMENT Goals

Based on your inventory and community needs, what 3 skills will you focus on developing?

1.
2.

3.

For each skill, what specific competency level do you want to achieve?

1.

2.

3.

Section C: Learning Plan

Skill	Learning Resources	Practice Opportunities	Timeline	Success Measures

Section D: Community Application

How will you use your developed skills to serve your community?

1.

2.

3.

Journal Prompt 8.1: Skills and Service

Reflect on these questions;

1. What needs in my community particularly move my heart?
2. How might developing my skills help me address those needs more effectively?
3. What fears or obstacles have prevented me from developing my skills more intentionally?

Chapter 9: Creating Multiple Streams of Income

The Steward's Diversification Strategy

In Ecclesiastes 11:2, we are advised thus, "Invest in seven ventures, yes, in eight as you do not know what disaster may come upon the land".

Developing multiple income streams is a practical expression of the biblical wisdom of diversification. It creates financial resilience that allows you to weather economic uncertainties while increasing your capacity for generosity and kingdom investment. Rather than relying on a single source of income, the wise steward develops multiple streams that align with their skills, values and calling.

The Biblical Case for Multiple Income Streams

Scripture consistently commends wisdom, diligence and preparation;

- The Proverbs 31 woman had multiple enterprises (v. 16, 18, 24)
- Ecclesiastes recommends diversification (11:2)
- Paul continued tent making while ministering (Acts 18:3)
- Joseph stored during plenty for coming famine (Genesis 41)

Multiple income streams provide;

- **Reduced Vulnerability**

Protection against job loss or industry downturns

- **Increased Generosity Capacity**

More resources to give

- **Ministry Funding**

Resources for kingdom projects

- **Skill Utilization**

Opportunities to use diverse gifts

- **Flexibility**

  Ability to respond to God's leading

Types of Income Streams
Income streams generally fall into three categories:

1. **Active Income**

   Trading time for money such as from employment, consulting, freelancing

1. **Portfolio Income**

   Earnings from investments such as dividends, interest, capital gains

1. **Passive Income**

   Revenue from assets you create or acquire such as rental properties, digital products, royalties

A healthy financial ecosystem includes all three types, though the mix will vary based on your season of life and specific calling.

Developing Income Streams Aligned with Your Values

Not all income opportunities align with biblical values or your specific calling. When evaluating potential income streams, consider

- **Ethical Alignment**: Does this opportunity honor God and serve people?
- **Time Commitment**: How does this fit with my primary responsibilities?
- **Skill Alignment**: Does this use my God-given abilities?
- **Ministry Compatibility**: Does this support or hinder my spiritual life and ministry?
- **Community Impact**: Does this benefit or harm my community?

The goal is not simply more income but income that supports your overall life mission.

Practical Steps for Developing Income Streams

Creating additional income streams requires intentionality;

1. **Start with Your Skills**

What valuable abilities do you already possess?

1. **Identify Market Needs**

What problems can you solve for others?

1. **Begin Small**

Test ideas with minimal investment

1. **Reinvest Early Earnings**

Fund growth before increasing personal spending

1. **Systematize Successful Ventures**

Create processes that do not depend solely on you

1. **Diversify Gradually**

Add streams as you have capacity

Keeping in mind that most successful income streams begin as side ventures while maintaining the primary employment.

Balancing Multiple Responsibilities

Managing multiple income streams requires wisdom to avoid burnout and neglect of important relationships. The goal is sustainable diversification that enhances rather than diminishes your life.

- **Time Blocking**: Dedicate specific times for different income activities

- **Delegation**: Outsource tasks that others can do better or more cheaply
- **Automation**: Use technology to handle repetitive tasks
- **Regular Evaluation**: Quarterly review of what is working and what is not
- **Sabbath Rest**: Maintain regular rest as spiritual obedience

Prayer for Income Diversification

"Provider God, You own all resources and faithfully supply our needs. Give me wisdom to develop multiple income streams that honor you. Guide me to opportunities that align with my skills and values. Protect me from greed and overwork in pursuing additional income. Help me balance multiple responsibilities without neglecting what matters most. May increased resources lead to increased generosity and kingdom impact. Amen".

Worksheet 9.1: Income Stream Development Plan

Purpose: To identify and develop multiple income streams aligned with your values and skills.

Section A: Current Income Assessment

Primary Income Sources:

1. Source: ______________________ Monthly Amount: $__________
2. Source: ______________________ Monthly Amount: $__________

Secondary Income Sources:

1. Source: ______________________ Monthly Amount: $__________
2. Source: ______________________ Monthly Amount: $__________

Total Monthly Income: $__________

Section B: Potential Income Streams

Based on your skills and market needs, list 3-5 potential income streams;

1.

2.

3.

4.

5.

Section C: Income Stream Evaluation

For each potential stream, evaluate;

Stream	Alignment with Values (1-5)	Startup Effort (1-5)	Income Potential	Timeline

Section D: Implementation Plan

Choose your top 1-2 income streams to develop first;

Stream 1: ____________________________

First 3 steps:

1.

2.

3.

Stream 2: ____________________________

First 3 steps:

1.

2.

3.

Journal Prompt 9.1: Income and Values

Reflect on these questions;

1. How do my current income sources align with my values and calling?
2. What fears or concerns come up when I think about developing additional income streams?
3. How might additional income increase my capacity for generosity and kingdom impact?

CHAPTER 10: THE STEWARD'S Investments

Growing Resources for Kingdom Impact

In Mathew 25:21, it is said "His master replied, 'Well done, good and faithful servant! You have been faithful with a few things; I will put you in charge of many things. Come and share your master's happiness!"

Investing, viewed through the lens of stewardship, involves putting resources to work for future kingdom impact. It represents a long-term perspective that acknowledges our responsibility to grow what we have been given for the benefit of future generations and future needs.

Biblical investing therefore prioritizes patience over speculation, values alignment over mere returns and eternal perspective over temporary gain.

The Theology of Investing

The Parable of the Talents in Matthew 25:14-30, provides foundational principles for

Investing as stewardship;

- **Ownership**

The resources belong to God, not us

- **Entrustment**

God gives different amounts according to our capacity and or calling

- **Expectation**

God expects multiplication of what He has entrusted

- **Accountability**

We will give account for our stewardship

- **Reward**

Faithful stewardship leads to greater responsibility and joy

INVESTING BECOMES PROBLEMATIC when it crosses into gambling/ speculation as it reflects greed (get-rich-quick mentality) or consumes our attention and stirs anxiety about returns. The key is maintaining proper perspective, seeing investing as a means of stewardship rather than an end in itself.

Biblical Investment Principles

Several principles should guide the steward's investment approach;

1. **Diversification**: "Invest in seven ventures, yes, in eight" (Ecclesiastes 11:2)
2. **Due Diligence**: "The prudent understand their way" (Proverbs 14:8)
3. **Long-Term Perspective**: "Steadfastness" (James 1:2-4)
4. **Ethical Alignment**: "Whatever is true, noble, right..." (Philippians 4:8)
5. **Contentment**: "Godliness with contentment is great gain" (1 Timothy 6:6)

These principles lead to an investment approach characterized by wisdom, patience and values alignment rather than speculation or greed.

Investment Vehicles and Strategies

Common investment options include:

1. **Retirement Accounts**: Tax-advantaged accounts for long-term savings
2. **Brokerage Accounts**: Regular investment accounts with more flexibility
3. **Real Estate**: Rental properties or REITs
4. **Business Ownership**: Starting or investing in businesses
5. **Values-Based Funds**: Investments screened for ethical alignment

A simple, effective strategy for most stewards involves;

- Regular contributions regardless of market conditions
- Broad diversification through low-cost index funds
- Long-term perspective without reaction to short-term fluctuations
- Periodic rebalancing to maintain target allocations

Values-Based Investing

The faithful investor recognizes that all investment involves moral choice, that is, where we place our money either supports or undermines various aspects of God's good creation. Values-based investing considers;

- **Negative Screening**

Avoiding companies involved in harmful activities

- **Positive Screening**

Seeking companies that contribute positively

- **Impact Investing**

Directing capital to address specific social or environmental issues

- **Shareholder Advocacy**

Using ownership to influence corporate behavior

While perfect alignment is impossible in a fallen world, we can thoughtfully direct capital toward activities that align with our God given values.

Investment and Generosity

A biblical approach to investing maintains generosity as a central goal. Strategies include;

- **Generous Current Giving**

  Maintaining generous giving while building investments

- **Appreciated Asset Gifting**

  Donating appreciated investments to avoid capital gains

- **Donor-Advised Funds**

  Creating vehicles for strategic giving

- **Estate Planning**

  Ensuring resources continue supporting kingdom work after we are gone

This approach ensures that investing serves generosity rather than replaces it.

Prayer for Investment Wisdom

"Eternal God, You own all things and entrust resources to your children for stewardship. Give me wisdom to invest in ways that honor you and serve your purposes. Protect me from greed, speculation and anxiety about returns. Guide me to investments that align with your values. Help me maintain perspective, investing for eternity rather than only for time. May the growth of resources lead to increased kingdom impact. Amen".

Worksheet 10.1: Investment Policy Statement

Purpose: To create a personal investment constitution that guides your decisions.

Section A: Investment Philosophy

My investment approach will be characterized by;

[ ] Long-term perspective

[ ] Broad diversification

[ ] Values alignment

[ ] Regular contributions

[ ] Other: ______________________________

Section B: Financial Goals

Short-Term Goals (1-3 years):

1.

2.

Medium-Term Goals (3-10 years):

1.

2.

Long-Term Goals (10+ years):

1.

2.

Section C: Asset Allocation

Target allocation for my investment portfolio:

- Stocks: ____________%
- Bonds: ____________%
- Real Estate: ____________%
- Cash: ____________%
- Other: ____________%

Section D: Values Guidelines

Companies/industries I will avoid investing in;

1.

2.

3.

Positive characteristics I will seek in investments;

1.
2.
3.

Section E: Implementation Plan

Investment accounts I will use;

1.
2.
3.

Regular contribution amount: $__________ per __________

Rebalancing frequency: ____________________________

Journal Prompt 10.1: Investing and Eternity

Reflect on these questions;

1. How does eternity perspective affect how I think about investing?
2. What concerns do I have about aligning my investments with my values?
3. How can I ensure that investing serves generosity rather than replaces it?

Chapter 11: Generosity Transformed

GIVING AS WORSHIP AND Warfare

In 2 Corinthians 9:7, it is written "Each of you should give what you have decided in your heart to give, not reluctantly or under compulsion, for God loves a cheerful giver".

Generosity represents the ultimate expression of financial wholeness, that is, it is the point where our stewardship culminates in joyful distribution.

When we understand that everything we have belongs to God, giving transforms from reluctant obligation to joyful participation in God's work in the world. Generosity realigns our hearts with God's heart, breaking the power of materialism and awakening us to the profound joy of sharing.

The Theology of Generosity

Biblical generosity flows from understanding several key truths;

- **God's Nature**: God is the ultimate giver (John 3:16)
- **Our Identity**: We are receivers who become conduits of God's generosity
- **Kingdom Economy**: Giving stores up treasure in heaven (Matthew 6:19-21)
- **Spiritual Warfare**: Generosity breaks the power of mammon (Matthew 6:24)
- **Worship**: Giving is an act of worship that honors God (Philippians 4:18)

When we grasp these truths, generosity becomes not something we do but something we are the natural overflow of hearts transformed by God's generosity toward us.

The Transformative Power of Generosity

Generosity transforms both the giver and receiver:

For the Giver:

- Breaks the power of materialism and greed
- Cultivates trust in God's provision
- Brings joy and fulfillment
- Aligns our hearts with God's heart
- Stores up eternal treasure

For the Receiver:

- Meets practical needs
- Demonstrates God's love tangibly
- Encourages faith and hope
- Can transform life circumstances

For the Community:

- Models alternative values to consumerism
- Strengthens community bonds
- Demonstrates kingdom reality

Dimensions of Biblical Generosity

Biblical generosity encompasses multiple dimensions;

1. **Tithing**: The foundational practice of giving the first tenth to God's work
2. **Almsgiving**: Compassionate giving to those in need
3. **Hospitality**: Generous sharing of home and resources
4. **Sacrificial Giving**: Giving beyond what is comfortable
5. **Spontaneous Giving**: Responsive generosity to immediate needs
6. **Strategic Giving**: Thoughtful support of kingdom initiatives

Each dimension addresses different aspects of our hearts and different needs in the world.

Developing a Generous Lifestyle

Cultivating generosity involves both practical steps and heart transformation;

Practical Steps:

- **Start with Tithing**: Make giving the first financial priority
- **Automate Giving**: Set up regular transfers to make generosity consistent
- **Create a Generosity Fund**: Set aside money specifically for spontaneous giving
- **Practice Incremental Increase**: Gradually increase giving percentage over time
- **Give Beyond Money**: Generously share time, skills and possessions

Heart Transformation:

- **Meditate on God's Generosity**: Regularly reflect on all God has given you
- **Pray for a Generous Heart**: Ask God to make you more generous
- **Celebrate Giving**: Thank God for the privilege of giving
- **Share Stories**: Tell others about the joy of generosity

Generosity as Spiritual Warfare

In a world dominated by mammon, the spirit of materialism and greed, generosity becomes a powerful weapon of spiritual warfare. Every generous act;

- Declares that God, not money, is our God and provider
- Demonstrates kingdom values in a materialistic world
- Breaks the power of greed, selfishness, self-centeredness and fear in our own hearts
- Testifies to a better way of living
- Stores up eternal treasure that cannot be destroyed

When we give generously, we participate in God's work of redeeming the economic systems of this world.

Prayer for a Generous Heart

"Generous Father, You gave your most precious treasure, your Son for our salvation.

Transform our hearts to reflect your generous nature. Break the power of greed and fear in our lives. Give us joy in giving and wisdom in distribution. Make us conduits of your blessing to others. May our generosity declare your goodness and advance your kingdom. Amen".

Worksheet 11.1: Generosity Plan and Journal

Purpose: To develop a comprehensive approach to generosity and track its impact.

Section A: Generosity Assessment

Current giving percentage of income: __________%

How would I describe my attitude toward giving?

[ ] Cheerful [ ] Reluctant [ ] Anxious [ ] Obligated [ ] Joyful

What fears or concerns limit my generosity?

1.

2.

3.

Section B: Generosity Goals

Tithing Goal:

- Percentage: __________%
- Amount: $__________ monthly

Beyond-Tithing Giving:

- Percentage: __________%
- Amount: $__________ monthly

Spontaneous Giving Fund:

- Monthly amount: $__________

Section C: Generosity Distribution

How will I distribute my giving?

Category	Percentage	Monthly Amount	Organizations/Recipients
Local Church			
Missions			
Compassion			
Other			

Section D: Generosity Journal

Use this section to record giving and reflect on the experience:

Date	Amount	To Whom/Purpose	Prayer	Reflections

Journal Prompt 11.1: The Joy of Giving

Reflect on these questions;

1. What has been my most joyful giving experience? Why was it joyful?
2. What fears or concerns typically arise when I consider increasing my giving?
3. How has generosity transformed my relationship with money and with God?

Volume IV: Advanced Stewardship for Lasting Impact

Chapter 12: Entrepreneurial Stewardship

BUILDING BUSINESSES That Bless

In Colossians 3:23 scripture states, "Whatever you do, work at it with all your heart, as working for the Lord, not for human masters".

Entrepreneurship represents a powerful avenue for stewardship that extends beyond personal finance to creating value, providing employment and solving problems in our communities. When approached with a stewardship mindset, business ownership becomes a platform for kingdom impact that can far exceed what is possible through individual effort alone.

The Theology of Entrepreneurship

God is the ultimate entrepreneur, the Creator who brought order from chaos and continues to sustain and redeem His creation. As image-bearers, we participate in this creative work through entrepreneurial ventures that;

- **Create Value**

Developing products and services that meet real needs

- **Provide Employment**

Offering meaningful work and fair compensation

- **Solve Problems**

Addressing challenges in our communities

- **Model Kingdom Values**

Demonstrating alternative ways of doing business

- **Generate Resources**

Creating wealth that can fund kingdom initiatives

Entrepreneurship becomes sacred when motivated by service rather than selfishness, when guided by biblical values rather than mere profit and when pursued for God's glory rather than personal gain.

Identifying Kingdom Business Opportunities

Kingdom-minded entrepreneurs look for opportunities that align with several criteria;

1. **Address Real Needs**

Solving genuine problems rather than creating artificial wants

1. **Leverage Personal Passion**

Engaging areas where you feel called and energized

1. **Utilize God-Given Skills**

Employing the unique abilities God has given you

1. **Serve Underserved Communities**

Focusing on marginalized or overlooked populations

1. **Promote Human Flourishing**

Contributing to people's physical, spiritual and emotional well-being

The most sustainable kingdom businesses often emerge from the intersection of market needs, personal passion and kingdom mission.

Business Models for Kingdom Impact

Various business models can advance kingdom values:

1. **For-Profit with Mission**

Traditional businesses that integrate social responsibility

1. **Social Enterprises**

Businesses designed specifically to address social problems

1. **Cooperatives**

Worker or customer-owned businesses that share benefits broadly

1. **Hybrid Models**

Combining for-profit and nonprofit elements

The right model depends on your specific calling, community context and the problem you are addressing.

Biblical Business Practices

Kingdom businesses should reflect God's character through;

- **Excellence**: Producing quality work that honors God
- **Integrity**: Absolute honesty in all dealings
- **Justice**: Fair treatment of employees, customers and suppliers
- **Generosity**: Sharing profits with employees and community
- **Sabbath Rhythm**: Building rest into business operations
- **Servant Leadership**: Leading by serving rather than dominating

These practices become a powerful witness to God's kingdom in the marketplace.

Funding Kingdom Ventures

Securing funding requires both practical wisdom and spiritual discernment:

1. **Bootstrapping**: Self-funding through personal savings and revenue
2. **Kingdom Investors**: Seeking investors who share your values and mission
3. **Crowdfunding**: Raising small amounts from many supporters
4. **Grants and Competitions**: Applying for mission-aligned funding opportunities
5. **Traditional Financing**: Using conventional loans while maintaining values

Each funding source comes with different advantages and challenges that must be weighed prayerfully.

Prayer for Entrepreneurial Stewardship

"Creator God, You spoke worlds into existence and continue to sustain all things.

Give me wisdom to identify business opportunities that serve your purposes. Grant me courage to take faith-filled risks and perseverance to overcome obstacles. Help me build a business that reflects your character and advances your kingdom. May every aspect, from products to profits honor you and bless others. Amen".

Worksheet 12.1: Kingdom Business Plan

Purpose: To develop a business concept that integrates kingdom values and practical viability.

Section A: Business Concept

Core Idea

What product or service will you provide?

Target Market

Who will you serve?

Kingdom Impact

How will this business advance God's purposes?

Section B: Value Proposition

Problem Solved

What need does your business address?

Solution Offered

How does your business meet this need?

Competitive Advantage

What makes your approach unique and better?

SECTION C: OPERATIONS Plan

Key Activities

What main tasks will the business perform?

Resources Needed

What equipment, space or technology is required?

Team Requirements

What skills and roles are needed?

Section D: Financial Projections

Startup Costs

Itemize initial investment required

Revenue Model

How will the business generate income?

Profit Distribution Plan

How will profits be allocated between

- Reinvestment: ___________%
- Owner compensation: ___________%
- Employee bonuses: ___________%
- Generosity: ___________%
- Other: ___________%

Section E: Kingdom Metrics

How will you measure success beyond financial returns?

1.
2.
3.

JOURNAL PROMPT 12.1: Business as Ministry

Reflect on these questions;

1. How can my business become an expression of God's love for my community?
2. What fears or concerns do I have about integrating faith and business?
3. How might my business model need to differ from conventional approaches to reflect kingdom values?

Chapter 13: Legacy and Estate Planning

STEWARDSHIP BEYOND Your Lifetime

It is well written in Proverbs 13:22 that, "A good person leaves an inheritance for their children's children".

Estate planning is thus an ultimate act of stewardship that is, ensuring that the resources God has entrusted to you continue serving His purposes after you are gone. It represents a long-term perspective that acknowledges our temporary role as managers of God's eternal resources.

The Theology of Legacy

Scripture presents several important principles about legacy;

- **Temporary Stewardship**

  We brought nothing into the world and take nothing out (1 Timothy 6:7)

- **Multi-Generational Vision**

  God's covenant extends to a thousand generations (Deuteronomy 7:9)

- **Intentional Planning**

  The wise give thought to their ways (Proverbs 14:8)

- **Family Responsibility**

Providing for relatives is an expression of faith (1 Timothy 5:8)

Legacy planning becomes an act of worship when motivated by love for God and others rather than by pride or control.

Essential Estate Planning Documents
Every steward should have these basic documents;

1. **Will**: Directs distribution of assets and names guardians for minor children
2. **Living Will**: Specifies healthcare wishes if you cannot communicate
3. **Power of Attorney**: Authorizes someone to handle financial matters if you are incapacitated
4. **Healthcare Proxy**: Names someone to make medical decisions on your behalf
5. **Letter of Instruction**: Provides guidance not covered in legal documents

These documents ensure your wishes are honored and prevent confusion or conflict among loved ones.

Kingdom-Minded Estate Distribution
A stewardship approach to estate distribution considers;

1. **Family Needs**: Providing for spouses, children and dependent relatives
2. **Kingdom Advancement**: Designating portions for ministry and charity
3. **Values Transmission**: Including instructions or letters about spiritual heritage
4. **Tax Efficiency**: Maximizing what passes to heirs and ministry
5. **Flexibility**: Building in adaptability for changing circumstances

Many stewards use a proportional approach, such as dividing assets equally between family and kingdom work.

Trusts and Other Tools
Various tools can enhance your estate plan:

1. **Revocable Living Trust**

Avoids probate and provides management during incapacity

1. **Irrevocable Trusts**

Provide asset protection and tax benefits

1. **Donor-Advised Funds**

Simplify charitable giving during life and after death

1. **Charitable Remainder Trusts**

Provide income with remainder going to ministry

1. **Family Limited Partnerships**

Facilitate business succession and asset protection

Consulting with Christian estate planning professionals can help identify the right tools for your situation.

Communicating Your Legacy

Effective legacy planning includes communication:

1. **Family Meetings**: Discussing plans and values with heirs
2. **Ethical Will**: Writing a letter explaining your spiritual values and hopes
3. **Mentoring**: Investing in the next generation's character and capabilities
4. **Document Organization**: Ensuring loved ones can find important papers
5. **Professional Introduction**: Connecting heirs with advisors who can help them

This communication honors relationships and prepares heirs to be good stewards.

Prayer for Legacy Planning

"Eternal God, You exist outside of time yet care about each generation. Give me wisdom to plan for what happens after I pass on. Help me balance providing for family with advancing your kingdom. Guide me to create a legacy that honors you and blesses others. May the resources I have stewarded continue bearing fruit for your glory. Amen".

Worksheet 13.1: Legacy Planning Guide

Purpose: To create a comprehensive legacy plan that reflects your values.

Section A: Personal Information

Key Advisors:

- Attorney: ______________________
- Financial Advisor: ______________________
- Accountant: ______________________
- Spiritual Advisor: ______________________

Important Documents Location:

- Will: ______________________
- Trust: ______________________
- Insurance Policies: ______________________
- Investment Statements: ______________________

Section B: Asset Distribution Plan

List major assets and intended distribution:

Asset	Current Value	Primary Beneficiary	Secondary Beneficiary

Section C: Charitable Bequests

Organizations to Support:

1. ______________________ Amount/Percentage: ___________
2. ______________________ Amount/Percentage: ___________
3. ______________________ Amount/Percentage: ___________

Section D: Personal Wishes

Guardianship

If minor children, preferred guardian: ______________________

Healthcare Directives

Life support preferences: ______________________

Funeral Arrangements

Basic preferences: ______________________

Section E: Ethical Will

What values and spiritual heritage do you want to pass on?

What advice or blessings do you want to leave for loved ones?

Journal Prompt 13.1: Eternal Perspective

Reflect on these questions;

1. How does remembering my mortality affect how I view my possessions?
2. What values do I most want to pass on to the next generation?
3. How can I use estate planning as an act of worship and trust in God's ongoing work?

Chapter 14: Teaching the Next Generation

RAISING FAITHFUL STEWARDS

Proverbs 22:6 advises parents thus, "Start children off on the way they should go and even when they are old they will not turn from it".

One of our most important stewardship responsibilities is training the next generation to handle resources wisely. In a culture saturated with consumerism and materialism, teaching biblical financial principles becomes countercultural discipleship that can shape character and eternal destiny.

The Importance of Financial Discipleship

Teaching children about money:

- **Shapes Character**

Develops diligence, generosity and self-control

- **Prevents Future Bondage**

Equips them to avoid debt and financial stress

- **Prepares for Responsibility**

Readies them to manage God's resources

- **Transmits Values**

Communicates what is truly important

- **Strengthens Faith**

Demonstrates God's faithfulness in practical ways

Financial teaching is most effective when integrated into normal life rather than treated as a separate subject.

Age-Appropriate Financial Teaching
Ages 3-5: Basic Concepts

- Identifying coins and their values
- Understanding that money is exchanged for goods
- Simple saving for small purchases
- Introduction to giving at church

Ages 6-12: Foundation Building

- Allowance tied to responsibilities
- Three-jar system: Give, Save, Spend
- Comparison shopping
- Basic entrepreneurship (lemonade stands, etc.)
- Introduction to tithing

Ages 13-18: Advanced Preparation

- Budgeting for clothing and entertainment
- Part-time employment
- Banking and saving for larger goals
- Introduction to investing
- Discernment about advertising and consumerism

Young Adults: Launching Well

- Comprehensive budgeting
- Debt avoidance strategies
- Insurance basics
- Retirement account introduction
- Generosity planning

TEACHING METHODS THAT Work

Effective financial discipleship uses multiple approaches;

1. **Modeling**: Demonstrating wise financial habits

2. **Conversation**: Discussing money matters openly and appropriately
3. **Practice**: Providing hands-on experience with money
4. **Storytelling**: Sharing both successes and failures
5. **Mentoring**: Involving other trusted adults in teaching
6. **Formal Instruction**: Using curricula or structured programs

The goal is not just information transfer but character formation.

Handling Special Challenges

Common challenges require thoughtful approaches;

1. **Wealthy Families**: Preventing entitlement and developing gratitude
2. **Limited Resources**: Teaching contentment and creativity
3. **Blended Families**: Navigating different financial cultures and expectations
4. **Special Needs Children**: Adapting teaching for different capabilities
5. **Adult Children in Crisis**: Providing help without enabling dependency

Each situation requires prayerful wisdom and sometimes professional guidance.

Creating a Family Financial Culture

Intentional families develop distinctive financial cultures characterized by;

1. **Shared Values**: Clear understanding of what matters most
2. **Open Communication**: Regular discussion about money matters
3. **Generosity Traditions**: Established patterns of giving together
4. **Work Ethic**: Appreciation for meaningful work

1. **Contentment**: Resistance to comparison and consumerism
2. **Eternal Perspective**: Regular reminder that life is more than possessions

This culture becomes the soil in which financial wisdom grows naturally.

Prayer for the Next Generation

"Faithful God, You care about each generation and desire godly offspring. Give me wisdom to teach financial principles that honor you. Help me model faithful stewardship in my own life. Protect my children from materialism and entitlement. Make them generous, wise and content stewards of your resources. May they use whatever you entrust to them for your glory. Amen".

Worksheet 14.1: Family Financial Discipleship Plan

Purpose: To create an intentional plan for teaching biblical stewardship to the next generation.

Section A: Current Assessment

Children/Ages:

1. ______________________ Age: _____
2. ______________________ Age: _____
3. ______________________ Age: _____

Current Financial Practices:

- Allowance: [ ] Yes [ ] No Amount: $___________
- Chores tied to money: [ ] Yes [ ] No
- Regular giving: [ ] Yes [ ] No
- Saving required: [ ] Yes [ ] No

Section B: Age-Appropriate Goals

For each child, list 2-3 financial skills to develop this year:

Child 1: ______________________

1.
2.
3.

Child 2: ______________________

1.
2.
3.

Child 3: ______________________

1.
2.
3.

Section C: Teaching Methods

What methods will you use to teach financial principles?

[ ] Allowance system [ ] Family meetings [ ] Shopping lessons
[ ] Entrepreneurship projects [ ] Book/curriculum [ ] Other: ___________

Section D: Family Financial Traditions

What traditions will you establish around money?

- Giving: ____________________________
- Saving: ____________________________
- Celebrating: ____________________________
- Discussing: ____________________________

SECTION E: RESOURCES Needed

What tools or resources will help your teaching?

1.
2.
3.

Journal Prompt 14.1: Generational Stewardship

Reflect on these questions;

1. What financial messages did I receive growing up? How do I want to replicate or change these for the next generation?
2. What concerns do I have about teaching my children about money?
3. How can I make financial discipleship a natural part of our family life rather than another task?

Chapter 15: The Financially Whole Life

INTEGRATING ALL WE Are Becoming

"So whether you eat or drink or whatever you do, do it all for the glory of God" as written in 1 Corinthians 10:31.

Financial wholeness is not a destination but a continuous journey of integration, that is, the bringing together of our spiritual values, our practical decisions, our personal mission and our community relationships. The financially whole person experiences a harmonious alignment between belief and practice, between faith and finance, between calling and capacity.

The Integrated Life

Financial wholeness manifests in several dimensions;

1. **Spiritual Integration**

Financial decisions flow naturally from relationship with God

1. **Relational Harmony**

Money matters strengthen rather than strain important relationships

1. **Emotional Peace**

Financial situations produce contentment rather than anxiety

1. **Practical Competence**

Effective management of day-to-day financial matters

1. **Generous Orientation**

Natural inclination toward sharing and serving

1. **Eternal Perspective**

Understanding that life is more than possessions

This integration transforms money from a source of stress to a tool for worship.

DAILY PRACTICES OF Financial Wholeness

Financially whole people typically practice;

1. **Regular Financial Review**: Weekly or monthly check-ins on spending and goals
2. **Prayerful Decision-Making**: Bringing financial choices to God in prayer
3. **Gratitude Journaling**: Regularly noting God's provision
4. **Generous Giving**: Consistent, joyful sharing of resources
5. **Contentment Cultivation**: Practicing appreciation for what they have
6. **Continuous Learning**: Ongoing financial education and skill development
7. **Accountability Relationships**: Trusted friends who provide perspective and challenge

These practices maintain alignment between values and financial reality.

Seasons of Financial Life

Financial wholeness looks different in various life stages;

Young Adults (20s-30s):

- Focus: Foundation building, debt avoidance, skill development

- Challenges: Lower income, establishing career, starting family
- Opportunities: Developing good habits early, time for compound growth

Mid-Life (40s-50s):

- Focus: Wealth building, education funding, career advancement
- Challenges: Multiple financial demands, aging parents, college costs
- Opportunities: Higher earning potential, established networks

PRE-RETIREMENT (50S-60s):

- Focus: Retirement preparation, debt elimination, legacy planning
- Challenges: Health issues, caring for parents, empty nest adjustments
- Opportunities: Wisdom and experience, often peak earnings

Retirement (65+):

- Focus: Sustainable distributions, generosity, passing on wisdom
- Challenges: Healthcare costs, loss of spouse, cognitive decline
- Opportunities: Time for volunteering and mentoring, enjoying fruits of labor

Each season requires adjusting strategies while maintaining core principles.

Overcoming Setbacks and Challenges

Financially whole people develop resilience through;

1. **Emergency Preparedness**: Maintaining adequate savings for unexpected events
2. **Adaptability**: Willingness to adjust plans when circumstances change
3. **Perseverance**: Continuing faithful practices during difficult times
4. **Community Support**: Leaning on others during challenges
5. **Spiritual Foundation**: Trusting God's faithfulness regardless of situations

Setbacks become opportunities for growth rather than reasons for despair.

The Joy of Financial Wholeness

The ultimate reward of financial wholeness is freedom;

- **Freedom from Anxiety**: Peace that transcends circumstances
- **Freedom to Serve**: Capacity to respond to God's promptings
- **Freedom to Enjoy**: Ability to appreciate God's gifts without guilt

- **Freedom to Give**: Resources to bless others generously
- **Freedom to Focus**: Mental space for relationships and calling

This freedom reflects the abundant life Jesus promised (John 10:10).

Continuing the Journey

Financial wholeness is not a state we achieve but a direction we travel. The journey continues through;

1. **Lifelong Learning**: Always growing in wisdom and understanding
2. **Regular Course Correction**: Adjusting plans as life circumstances change
3. **Mentoring Others**: Sharing lessons learned with those coming behind
4. **Deepening Trust**: Growing in reliance on God's provision
5. **Expanding Generosity**: Increasing capacity and creativity in giving

The journey itself becomes an adventure in faithfulness.

Prayer for Continued Journey

"Faithful Guide, You have been with me through every step of this journey. Thank you for the progress made and lessons learned. Give me wisdom for the continued path ahead. Keep me from complacency in good times and despair in difficult ones. May my financial life increasingly reflect your character and advance your kingdom.

Until the day I hear, 'Well done, good and faithful servant' Amen".

Worksheet 15.1: Financial Wholeness Assessment

Purpose: To evaluate current financial wholeness and identify areas for continued growth.

Section A: Wholeness Dimensions Assessment

Rate yourself on each dimension (1 = needs significant work, 5 = fully whole):

Spiritual Integration: _____

- My financial decisions reflect my relationship with God
- I regularly bring financial matters to God in prayer
- I see money as a tool for worship rather than an end in itself

Relational Harmony: _____

- Money matters strengthen my important relationships
- I communicate openly about financial matters with appropriate people
- Financial decisions consider impact on others

Emotional Peace: _____

- I experience contentment regardless of financial circumstances
- Financial situations do not produce excessive anxiety
- I maintain perspective during market fluctuations or setbacks

Practical Competence: _____

- I effectively manage day-to-day financial matters
- I have systems that work for tracking and decision-making
- I'm continuing to grow in financial knowledge and skills

Generous Orientation: _____

- Giving comes naturally and joyfully
- I look for opportunities to share resources
- I am increasing in generosity over time

Eternal Perspective: _____

- I understand that life is more than possessions
- I'm investing in eternal treasure
- My financial decisions consider long-term impact

Section B: Growth Areas

Based on your assessment, identify 2-3 areas for focused growth;

1.

2.

3.

Section C: Action Plan

For each growth area, list specific steps;

Area 1: ______________________

Steps:

1.

2.

3.

Area 2: ______________________

Steps:

1.

2.

3.

Area 3: ______________________

Steps:

1.

2.

3.

SECTION D: SUPPORT System

Who will help me in this continued journey?

- Accountability partner: ______________________
- Professional advisors: ______________________

- Spiritual mentor: ______________________
- Other: ______________________

Journal Prompt 15.1: The Journey Ahead
Reflect on these questions;

1. What has been the most significant transformation in my financial life during this journey?
2. What area of financial wholeness do I most want to develop in the coming year?
3. How can I use my financial wholeness to bless others and honor God?

Chapter 16: The Theology of Abundance

MOVING FROM SCARCITY to Kingdom Economy

"And God is able to bless you abundantly, so that in all things at all times, having all that you need, you will abound in every good work" as written in 2 Corinthians 9:8 is worth remembering.

Understanding Kingdom Economics

The world operates on a scarcity mindset, that is, the belief that there is never enough. On the other hand, Kingdom economics is rooted in abundance, the recognition that our God owns everything and generously provides for His children.

Key Principles of Kingdom Abundance

1. **God's Unlimited Resources**

Our provision comes from God's unlimited storehouse, not limited human systems

1. **Multiplication Mentality**

God multiplies what we faithfully steward

1. **Firstfruits Living**

Giving first demonstrates trust in ongoing provision

1. **Storehouse Principle**

God blesses us to be blessings to others

1. **Eternal Perspective**

True wealth is measured in eternal impact, not temporal accumulation

Practicing Abundance Consciousness

- Begin each day with declarations of God's faithfulness
- Keep a "Provision Journal" recording specific ways God provides
- Practice "reverse tithing", for instance, giving 90% and living on 10% for a season
- Speak abundance over others' financial situations
- Regularly review God's faithfulness throughout Scripture and your life

Worksheet 16.1: Abundance Mindset Assessment

Scarcity Thinking Patterns to Identify

- "There's never enough"
- "I have to hoard to be safe"
- "If others have more, I have less"
- "I cannot afford to be generous right now"
- "Money is evil/dirty"

Abundance Declarations to Adopt

1. "My God supplies all my needs according to His riches"
2. "I am a conduit of God's blessing to others"
3. "There is always enough for God's purposes"
4. "My generosity makes room for more blessing"
5. "Money is a tool for kingdom advancement"

Abundance Practices for the Next 90 Days

1.
2.
3.

Chapter 17: Strategic Generosity

MAXIMUM IMPACT GIVING

Timothy 6:18-19 reminds us, "Command them to do good, to be rich in good deeds and to be generous and willing to share. In this way they will lay up treasure for themselves as a firm foundation for the coming age, so that they may take hold of the life that is truly life".

The Four Dimensions of Strategic Generosity

1. **Reactive Giving**

Responding to immediate needs as demonstrated by the Good Samaritan.

1. **Proactive Giving**

Systematic support of ongoing ministry, examples include regular tithing

1. **Strategic Giving**

Funding initiatives that address root causes such as justice ministries

1. **Legacy Giving**

Establishing ongoing funding streams such as endowments, foundations

Creating a Generosity Portfolio:

Just as you diversify investments, diversify your giving;

- 50% to local church and direct ministry
- 20% to compassion ministries addressing immediate needs
- 20% to justice ministries addressing systemic issues
- 10% to spontaneous, Spirit-led giving

Advanced Giving Vehicles:

1. **Donor-Advised Funds**: Simpler than private foundations with similar benefits
2. **Charitable Trusts**: Provide income while benefiting charity
3. **Private Foundations**: For those with significant assets to steward
4. **Mission-Driven Investments**: Investing in companies that align with values
5. **Microfinance Lending**: Supporting entrepreneurs in developing areas

Worksheet 17.1: Generosity Portfolio Assessment
Current Giving Distribution:

- Local Church: ___________%
- Compassion Ministries: ___________%
- Justice Ministries: ___________%
- Spontaneous Giving: ___________%
- Other: ___________%

Impact Evaluation:
Which giving brings the most:

- Joy: _______________________
- Eternal impact: _______________________
- Community transformation: _______________________

Strategic Adjustments:
1.
2.
3.

Chapter 18: Financial Discernment

HEARING GOD'S VOICE in Money Matters

Scripture reminds us in Isaiah 30:21 that God normally orders our steps, "Whether you turn to the right or to the left, your ears will hear a voice behind you, saying, 'This is the way; walk in it".

Developing Financial Discernment

Financial decisions involve more than spreadsheets and calculations. Financial decisions require spiritual discernment.

Questions for Discernment

1. **The Peace Test**: Does this decision bring God's peace?
2. **The Wisdom Test**: Does this align with biblical wisdom?
3. **The Counsel Test**: What do wise advisors say?
4. **The Timing Test**: Is this God's timing?
5. **The Motive Test**: Why do I really want this?
6. **The Generosity Test**: How does this affect my giving?
7. **The Legacy Test**: What message does this send to others?

Discerning God's Voice vs. Other Voices:

- God's voice brings peace; fear screams urgency
- God's voice aligns with Scripture; temptation twists it
- God's voice often requires faith; fear demands certainty
- God's voice focuses on others; selfishness focuses on self

WORKSHEET 18.1: FINANCIAL Decision Discernment Grid

Decision to Make: ______________________

Evaluation:

Question	Rating (1-5)	Notes
Peace Test		
Wisdom Test		
Counsel Test		
Timing Test		
Motive Test		
Generosity Test		
Legacy Test		

Overall Discernment: [ ] Proceed [ ] Wait [ ] Stop

Chapter 19: The Steward's Sabbath

Rhythms of Rest and Trust

“THEN HE SAID TO THEM, 'Watch out! Be on your guard against all kinds of greed, life does not consist in an abundance of possessions” in Luke 12:15.

Sabbath Economics

The Sabbath principle reminds us that our provision comes from God's work, not our own.

Sabbath Financial Practices

1. **Financial Sabbath Weekly**: 24 hours with no financial activity or worry
2. **Sabbath Year Planning**: Every 7 years, evaluate and reset financial systems
3. **Jubilee Mindset**: Regular debt forgiveness and fresh starts for others
4. **Firstfruits Giving**: Give before spending rather than from leftovers
5. **Trust Exercises**: Periodic practices that stretch your trust in God's provision

Sabbath Resistance

In a 24/7 economy, Sabbath practices resist:

- The tyranny of urgency
- The addiction to accumulation
- The illusion of control
- The worship of productivity

Worksheet 19.1: Sabbath Financial Plan
Weekly Sabbath Practices

- No checking accounts or financial apps: [ ] Yes [ ] No
- No discussing money matters: [ ] Yes [ ] No
- No shopping or online purchases: [ ] Yes [ ] No
- Replacement activities: ______________________

Annual Sabbath Evaluation (Every 7 Years)
Areas to examine

1. Spending patterns and priorities
2. Investment philosophy and vehicles
3. Giving strategies and recipients
4. Debt levels and types
5. Financial goals and purposes

Chapter 20: Creating Community Wealth

BEYOND PERSONAL STEWARDSHIP

"All the believers were one in heart and mind. No one claimed that any of their possessions was their own but they shared everything they had" as written in Acts 4:32.

The Economics of Kingdom Community

While personal stewardship is essential, God's vision includes community flourishing.

Models for Community Economic Development

1. **Kingdom Business Incubators**: Supporting Christian entrepreneurs
2. **Community Development Funds**: Pooled resources for local impact
3. **Skill-Sharing Networks**: Exchanging services without money
4. **Cooperative Ownership**: Worker-owned businesses
5. **Local Investment Clubs**: Kingdom-minded investors funding local ventures

Principles for Community Wealth Building

- Asset-based rather than need-based approach
- Multiplier effect, that is, money circulating locally
- Dignity through participation, not just receiving
- Sustainable models that do not create dependency
- Measurement of holistic flourishing, not just financial metrics

Worksheet 20.1: Community Wealth Assessment
Community Assets

- Underutilized skills: ______________________
- Unmet needs that could become enterprises: ______________________
- Available spaces: ______________________
- Potential investors: ______________________
- Kingdom-minded entrepreneurs: ______________________

Action Plan

1. Connect: ______________________ with ______________________
2. Start: ______________________
3. Fund: ______________________

Chapter 21: The Steward's Legacy

BEYOND MONEY TO ETERNAL Impact

"Then the King will say to those on his right, 'Come, you who are blessed by my Father, take your inheritance, the kingdom prepared for you since the creation of the world" in Matthew 25:34

What Really Lasts

As you mature in stewardship, you realize that the greatest legacy is not what you accumulate but what you impart.

Elements of an Eternal Legacy

1. **Spiritual Heritage**: Faith passed to the next generation
2. **Kingdom Values**: Biblical worldview regarding money and possessions
3. **Reproducing Stewards**: People you have mentored in faithfulness
4. **Eternal Investments**: Resources invested in heaven's bank
5. **Gospel Advance**: Financial support of eternal salvation

Legacy Planning Beyond the Will

- Ethical Will detailing values and beliefs
- Stewardship mentoring program
- Family mission statement
- Generosity traditions and rituals
- Story collection of God's faithfulness

Worksheet 21.1: Eternal Legacy Plan

Spiritual Heritage

How I will intentionally pass on faith:

1.
2.
3.

Values Transmission

Key money messages I want to leave:

1.
2.
3.

Reproduction Plan

People I will mentor in stewardship:

1.
2.
3.

Eternal Investments

Current giving with eternal impact: ______________________

Planned legacy giving: ______________________

Chapter 22: The Art of Contentment in a Consumer Culture

IN PHILIPPIANS 4:12, the writer wrote, "I know what it is to be in need and I know what it is to have plenty. I have learned the secret of being content in any and every situation, whether well fed or hungry, whether living in plenty or in want".

Cultivating Holy Dissatisfaction

Contentment is not complacency. It is finding satisfaction in God while maintaining holy dissatisfaction with the world's brokenness.

Practices for Contentment

1. **Gratitude Journaling**: Daily recording of blessings
2. **Comparison Fasting**: Periods without media that fuels discontent
3. **Enough Declarations**: Regular affirmation of God's sufficient provision
4. **Simple Living Experiments**: Temporary reductions to rediscover essentials
5. **Generosity as Therapy**: Giving as antidote to greed

Contentment While Pursuing Excellence

- Excellence honors God; perfectionism burdens people
- Contentment receives God's gifts; complacency ignores human responsibility
- Holy dissatisfaction fuels kingdom action; worldly discontent fuels selfish accumulation

Worksheet 22.1: Contentment Cultivation Plan
Gratitude Practices

- Morning thanksgiving: 3 things I'm grateful for
- Mealtime blessings that acknowledge provision
- Evening reflection on the day's gifts

Comparison Resistance

- Media to limit: ______________________
- Conversations to avoid: ______________________
- Truths to remember when tempted to compare: ______________________

Simple Living Experiments

- Next month's experiment: ______________________
- What I hope to learn: ______________________

Chapter 23: Financial Wholeness and the Great Commission

IN MATTHEW 28:19, WE are reminded, "Therefore go and make disciples of all nations, baptizing them in the name of the Father and of the Son and of the Holy Spirit".

Funding the Finishing of the Task

Financial wholeness is not an end in itself, it is meant to fuel the Great Commission. Hence, the need to explore how financially whole stewards can strategically support global disciple-making.

Strategic Global Investment

1. **Unreached Peoples**: Prioritizing those with least access to the gospel
2. **National Workers**: Supporting indigenous missionaries and church planters
3. **Leadership Development**: Training the next generation of global Christian leaders
4. **Business as Mission**: Creating sustainable witness in closed countries
5. **Scripture Translation**: Ensuring everyone has God's Word in their heart language

Principles for Global Stewardship

- Partnership rather than paternalism
- Sustainability rather than dependency
- Accountability and transparency
- Cultural sensitivity and humility
- Eternal impact measurement

Worksheet 23.1: Global Impact Plan
Current Global Giving

- Amount: $__________
- Percentage of total giving: __________%
- Regions supported: ____________________
- Strategies funded: ____________________

Growth Goals

- Increase global giving to __________% within __________ months
- Add support for: ____________________
- Visit field within next __________ years

Learning Plan

- Books to read about global missions: ____________________
- Conferences to attend: ____________________
- People to learn from: ____________________

Chapter 24: The Steward's Worship

FINANCIAL PRACTICES as Spiritual Disciplines

In Romans 12:1, it is written thus "Therefore, I urge you, brothers and sisters, in view of God's mercy, to offer your bodies as a living sacrifice, holy and pleasing to God, this is your true and proper worship"

The Sacramental Nature of Financial Practices

When offered to God, ordinary financial activities become extraordinary worship. Thus the need to address how to transform money management into spiritual formation.

Financial Practices as Spiritual Disciplines

1. **Budgeting as Trust**: Allocating resources in dependence on God
2. **Giving as Worship**: Offering back to God what is already His
3. **Saving as Hope**: Preparing for God's future purposes
4. **Investing as Faith**: Risking for kingdom advancement
5. **Spending as Stewardship**: Using resources for God's glory
6. **Earning as Service**: Work as ministry to others

Creating Financial Liturgies

- Morning offering of the day's work
- Mealtime gratitude for provision
- Giving as celebratory worship
- Monthly financial review as spiritual examination
- Year-end planning as consecration

WORKSHEET 24.1: FINANCIAL Worship Plan

Daily Financial Liturgies

- Morning: ______________________
- Mealtime: ______________________
- Evening: ______________________

Weekly Worship Practices

- Sabbath financial rest: [ ] Yes [ ] No
- Giving celebration: ______________________
- Financial review as worship: ______________________

Monthly Consecration

How I will offer this month's finances to God: ______________________

Chapter 25: Passing the Baton

MULTIPLYING STEWARDS for the Next Generation

In 2 Timothy 2:2, it is written, "And the things you have heard me say in the presence of many witnesses entrust to reliable people who will also be qualified to teach others".

The Multiplication Mandate

In conclusion, financial wholeness is not accumulation but multiplication. Financial wholeness is not just about managing resources well but raising up others who will do the same.

Creating a Stewardship Culture

1. **Modeling Transparency**: Being open about financial journey, both the successes and failures
2. **Intentional Teaching**: Creating structured learning opportunities
3. **Hands-on Mentoring**: Walking with others through real financial decisions
4. **Creating Systems**: Establishing ongoing stewardship development in your church or organization
5. **Celebrating Faithfulness**: Recognizing and rewarding good stewardship

Multiplication Metrics

- Number of people you have mentored in stewardship
- Stories of transformed financial lives
- Generosity multiplied through those you have taught
- Stewardship principles adopted by organizations you influence
- Eternal impact through reproduction

WORKSHEET 25.1: STEWARDSHIP Multiplication Plan

People to Mentor

1. Name: ______________________ Timeline: ______________________
2. Name: ______________________ Timeline: ______________________
3. Name: ______________________ Timeline: ______________________

Teaching Opportunities

- Class to teach: ______________________
- Workshop to offer: ______________________
- Writing to share: ______________________

Legacy Systems

- Stewardship program to establish: ______________________
- Funding for ongoing training: ______________________
- Materials to develop: ______________________

Volume V: The Steward's Toolbox - Resources for Lifelong Practice

INTRODUCTION TO THE Steward's Toolbox

The journey to financial wholeness is not a destination but a lifelong pilgrimage, a continuous process of learning, growing and practicing faithful stewardship. Thus the need for a stewardship workshops, a collection of resources, tools, templates, prayers and practices that you can return to again and again as your circumstances change and your stewardship capacity grows.

Section 1: Comprehensive Financial Worksheets

1.1 Annual Financial Health Assessment

Purpose: To conduct a thorough yearly review of your financial situation and stewardship practices.

Part A: Spiritual and Emotional Check-in

1. How has my relationship with money changed this past year?
2. What financial fears have I surrendered to God? What still needs surrender?
3. Where have I seen God's provision most clearly?
4. How has generosity brought me joy this year?

Part B: Financial Statement Review

- Net Worth Comparison (Current vs. Previous Year): $__________
- Debt Reduction Progress: $__________
- Savings/Investment Growth: $__________
- Giving Percentage: __________%

Part C: Goal Progress Assessment

Goal Set Last Year Status (Achieved/In Progress/Not Started) Lessons Learned

Part D: Year-Ahead Planning

- Financial priorities for coming year
  1.
  2.
  3.
- Skills to develop
  1.
  2.
- Giving goals
  1.
  2.

1.2 Monthly Financial Check-in Template

Date: ______________________

Gratitude Reflection

Three financial blessings from this month:

1.
2.
3.

Financial Review

- Total Income: $__________
- Total Giving: $__________ (__________%)
- Total Saving/Investing: $__________ (__________%)
- Total Spending: $__________
- Emergency Fund Balance: $__________
- Debt Balances: $__________

Notable Observations

- Surprises (unexpected income or expenses):
- Challenges faced:
- Victories celebrated:

Adjustments for Next Month

1.
2.
3.

Prayer Focus

Financial matters to bring before God:

1.3 Debt Freedom Tracker

Purpose: To visually track progress toward becoming debt-free.

Starting Total Debt: $__________

Target Debt-Free Date: ______________________

Debt Payoff Progress

Month Total Debt Amount Paid Milestones Reached

Visual Progress Chart

(Create a bar or thermometer chart to color in as debt decreases)

CELEBRATION PLAN

How I will celebrate when each debt is eliminated:

1. ______________________: Celebration: ______________________
2. ______________________: Celebration: ______________________
3. ______________________: Celebration: ______________________

1.4 Generosity Journal and Planner

Purpose: To track giving and reflect on the joy of generosity.

Annual Giving Goal: $__________ (__________% of income)

Monthly Giving Record:

Date	Amount	Recipient	Purpose	Prayer	Reflection

Generosity Impact Stories

Record how your giving made a difference:

1.
2.
3.

Future Giving Goals

Causes/organizations I want to support:

1.
2.
3.

Section 2: Prayer Guides for Financial Matters

2.1 Daily Financial Prayers

Morning Dedication

"Heavenly Father, I dedicate this day's work and wealth to you. May my labor honor you and my spending reflect your values. Guide my financial decisions today. Amen".

Mealtime Gratitude

"Thank you, Lord, for this food and for all your provision. Help me to be mindful of those who have less and generous with what you have given me. Amen".

Evening Reflection

"Lord, as I review this day, I thank you for your faithful provision. Forgive me where I have been wasteful or selfish. Help me to trust you more tomorrow. Amen".

2.2 Situation-Specific Prayers

When Facing Financial Decisions

"Wisdom-giving God, I bring this decision before you. Give me clarity to see the options, discernment to choose wisely and peace to trust your guidance. May this choice honor you and serve others. Amen".

During Financial Stress

"Prince of Peace, my heart is anxious about money. I release these worries to you and choose to trust your provision. Help me to take wise steps while resting in your care. Amen".

When Giving Generously

"Generous Father, thank you for the privilege of sharing what you have given me. Multiply this gift for your kingdom purposes. Use it to show someone your love today. Amen".

When Receiving Unexpected Provision:

"Thank you, Lord, for this unexpected blessing. Help me to receive it with gratitude and use it with wisdom. Show me how you want me to steward this gift. Amen".

2.3 SEASONAL FINANCIAL Prayers

New Year Prayer

"Eternal God, as I begin this new year, I commit my financial plans to you. Guide my goal-setting, direct my spending, and expand my generosity. May this year bring greater financial wholeness for your glory. Amen".

Tax Season Prayer

"Righteous God, as I review this year's finances, give me integrity in my reporting. Help me to be a good citizen while maintaining kingdom priorities. Give me peace about what I owe and wisdom for future planning. Amen".

Season of Giving Prayer

"Lord of all, in this season of giving, protect me from materialism and busyness. Help me to give thoughtfully and worship fully. May my spending and giving reflect the gift of Jesus. Amen".

Section 3: Financial Crisis Response Kit

3.1 Emergency Financial Assessment

Purpose: To evaluate your situation during a financial crisis and create an action plan.

Immediate Situation

- Nature of crisis: ______________________
- Severity (1-10): _____
- Duration expected: ______________________

Resources Available

- Emergency fund: $___________
- Available credit: $___________
- Assets that could be liquidated: $___________
- Insurance coverage: $___________

IMMEDIATE ACTION STEPS (Next 48 hours)

1.
2.

People to Notify

1. ______________________ (Reason: ______________________)
2. ______________________ (Reason: ______________________)
3. ______________________ (Reason: ______________________)

3.2 Crisis Budget Template

Purpose: To create a bare-bones budget during financial hardship.
Essential Expenses Only

- Housing: $___________
- Utilities: $___________
- Food: $___________
- Transportation: $___________
- Insurance: $___________
- Minimum Debt Payments: $___________

Total Essential Expenses: $___________
Income Sources

- Primary: $___________
- Secondary: $___________
- Assistance: $___________
- Other: $___________

Total Income: $___________
Surplus/Shortfall: $___________
Crisis Management Strategy

- Expenses to reduce: ______________________
- Payments to defer: ______________________
- Assistance to seek: ______________________
- Items to sell: ______________________

3.3 Crisis Communication Scripts

With Creditors

"Hello, I am experiencing a temporary financial hardship due to (brief explanation). I want to honor my obligation to you. What options do you have available to help me through this period?"

With Family

"I want to talk about our financial situation. We are facing (situation). Here is what I propose we do. How are you feeling about this? What ideas do you have?"

With Your Church/Community

"I am going through a difficult time financially and would appreciate your prayer support. If there are resources available to help, I would be grateful to know about them".

Section 4: Stewardship Development Resources
4.1 Recommended Reading List
Biblical Foundation

- Money, Possessions and Eternity by Randy Alcorn
- The Treasure Principle by Randy Alcorn
- Your Money Counts by Howard Dayton
- God and Money by Gregory Baumer and John Cortines

Practical Application

- The Total Money Makeover by Dave Ramsey
- The Simple Path to Wealth by JL Collins
- The Automatic Millionaire by David Bach
- The Millionaire Next Door by Thomas Stanley

Mindset and Behavior

- The Psychology of Money by Morgan Housel
- Atomic Habits by James Clear
- The 7 Habits of Highly Effective People by Stephen Covey

Entrepreneurship and Business

- Business for the Glory of God by Wayne Grudem
- The E-Myth Revisited by Michael Gerber
- Start with Why by Simon Sinek

4.2 Skill Development Planning Template

Purpose: To create a structured plan for developing income-generating skills.

Skill Selection

Primary skill to develop: ______________________

Why this skill? ______________________

Target proficiency level: ______________________

Timeline: ______________________

Learning Plan

Resources needed

1.
2.
3.

Practice opportunities

1.
2.
3.

Measurement of progress

1.
2.
3.

Application Strategy:

How will this skill generate income?

1.
2.

How will this skill serve others?

1.
2.

4.3 Networking for Stewardship Worksheet

Purpose: To build relationships that support your stewardship journey.

Current Network Assessment

People who model good stewardship

1.
2.
3.

People who need stewardship encouragement

1.
2.
3.

Professional advisors in my network

- Financial: ______________________
- Legal: ______________________
- Spiritual: ______________________

Network Growth Goals

People I would like to learn from

1.
2.

People I could mentor

1.
2.

Action Steps:

1. Schedule lunch with: ______________________
2. Attend event: ______________________
3. Join group: ______________________

Section 5: Legacy Planning Tools

5.1 Ethical Will Template

Purpose: To pass on values and spiritual heritage to the next generation.

My Spiritual Journey

Key moments in my relationship with God;

Lessons Learned About Money

What I wish I had known earlier;

What brought the most joy;

What I regret;

Values I Hope to Pass On

1.

2.

3.

Specific Blessings for Loved Ones:

(Write personal messages to family members)

My Hopes for Future Generations:

Spiritually;

Financially;

Relationally;

5.2 Stewardship Letter to Heirs

Purpose: To communicate your stewardship philosophy to those who will inherit from you.

Introduction

Why I am writing this letter;

MY STEWARDSHIP PHILOSOPHY

What I believe about money and possessions;

How I tried to live this out;

About Your Inheritance

My prayers for how you will use what I leave;

My hopes for what it will enable in your life;

Advice and Encouragement

Financial principles that served me well;

Spiritual practices that sustained me;

My Confidence

Why I trust God with your future:

Closing Blessing

(Personal blessing for the reader)

Section 6: Monthly Reflection Prompts

6.1 Financial Sabbath Questions

For Monthly Reflection

1. Where did I see God's provision most clearly this month?
2. What financial decision am I most grateful for?
3. Where did I struggle with contentment?
4. How did generosity bring me joy?
5. What needs to change next month?

6.2 Quarterly Deeper Reflection

Spiritual Examination

- How is my relationship with money affecting my relationship with God?
- What financial fears do I need to surrender?
- Where is God calling me to greater trust?

Practical Review:

- Are my financial systems working well?
- What habits need strengthening?
- What knowledge do I need to acquire?

Relational Check:

- How are money matters affecting my key relationships?
- Who can I encourage in their stewardship journey?
- Who do I need to ask for advice or accountability?

Section 7: Generosity Challenge Worksheets

7.1 30-Day Generosity Challenge

Purpose: To cultivate a more generous lifestyle through daily practices.

Daily Generosity Practices

1. Day 1-7: Write thank you notes to people who've blessed you
2. Day 8-14: Give small gifts anonymously
3. Day 15-21: Look for spontaneous giving opportunities
4. Day 22-30: Increase regular giving by 1%

Generosity Journal:

Date Act of Generosity Amount (if $) Reflection

Lessons Learned

What surprised me;

What brought the most joy;

What I want to continue;

7.2 Generosity Growth Plan

Purpose: To systematically increase giving over time.

Current Giving

Percentage of income: %

Amount monthly: $

Growth Goals:

Next 6 months: ___________%

Next year: ___________%

Next 5 years: ___________%

Steps to Increase Giving

1.

2.

3.

Causes to Support

Current:

Future:

Prayer for Generosity Growth:

"Lord, give me faith to increase my giving. Show me where to give and fill me with joy in giving. Amen".

Benediction

MY DEAR FELLOW STEWARD,

As we come to the end of this written journey, remember that your actual journey of financial wholeness continues. These tools and resources are now yours to use, adapt and share. May they serve you well as you grow in faithful stewardship.

Remember that financial wholeness is not about perfection but about direction, not about never making mistakes but about continually learning and growing. God is less concerned with the size of your portfolio than with the state of your heart.

As you continue your stewardship journey, may you experience increasingly:

- The peace that comes from trusting God's provision
- The joy that flows from generous giving
- The freedom that emerges from wise management
- The purpose that develops from aligned values
- The impact that grows from faithful stewardship

May you hear those wonderful words one day, "Well done, good and faithful servant! You have been faithful with a few things, I will put you in charge of many things. Come and share your master's happiness!" as written in Matthew 25:21.

Your fellow steward on the journey,
Irene Mugure Nderitu

The Unending Journey

BELOVED STEWARD,

In summary, like the prudent steward mentioned in Scripture, the journey to financial wholeness never ends this side of eternity.

Thus the need to further explore new depths of trust, faith, prayer, new dimensions of generosity to explore, new ways to align our resources with God's eternal purposes.

We witness what begins as basic money management becoming worship. What starts as debt reduction becoming freedom for greater service. What emerges as financial stability becoming a platform for kingdom impact.

Remember that financial wholeness is ultimately about wholeness, the integration of every area of life under Christ's lordship. As you continue this journey, may you experience the profound peace of trusting your Provider, the deep joy of generous giving and the lasting satisfaction of investing in what eternally matters.

Your stewardship journey is part of God's larger story of redemption. Your faithful management of resources, whether much or little becomes part of how God reveals His character to the world, provides for His children and advances His kingdom.

Well done, good and faithful steward. Continue the journey. There are greater things ahead.

Blessing

"MAY THE GOD OF ALL grace, who has called you to His eternal glory, restore, confirm, strengthen, and establish you as a faithful steward of His abundant resources. May you manage what He's entrusted with wisdom, distribute it with generosity, and celebrate it with joy until the day you hear, 'Well done, good and faithful servant. Enter into the joy of your Lord.' Amen."

www.ingramcontent.com/pod-product-compliance
Lightning Source LLC
LaVergne TN
LVHW022224200926
848481LV00006B/2105